Regulating
Wetlands
Protection

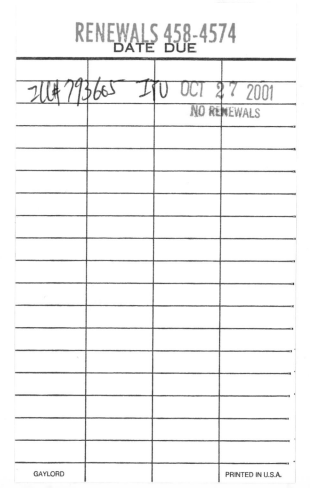

SUNY series in
Environmental Politics and Policy

Michael E. Kraft and Harlan Wilson, editors

Regulating Wetlands Protection

Environmental Federalism and the States

Ronald Keith Gaddie
and
James L. Regens

STATE UNIVERSITY OF NEW YORK PRESS

Cover photograph by Glenn Antizzo.

Production by Ruth Fisher
Marketing by Anne M. Valentine

Published by
State University of New York Press, Albany

For information, address the State University of New York Press,
State University Plaza, Albany, NY 12246

Library of Congress Cataloging-in-Publication Data

Gaddie, Ronald Keith.
    Regulating wetlands protection : environmental federalism and the
    States / Ronald Keith Gaddie and James L. Regens.
        p.   cm. — (SUNY series in environmental politics and policy)
    Includes bibliographical references and index.
    ISBN 0–7914–4349–3 (alk. paper.) — ISBN 0–7914–4350–7 (pbk. :
alk. paper)
        1. Wetland conservation—Government policy—United States.
    2. Wetlands—Management—Government policy—United States.
    3. Wetland conservation—Government policy—United States—States.
    4. Wetlands—Management—Government policy—United States—States.
    I. Regens, James L.   II. Series.
    QH76.G285   2000
    333.91´816´0973—dc21   99–15032
                                                                CIP

10 9 8 7 6 5 4 3 2 1

Contents

Preface

> The nation behaves well if it treats the natural resources as assets
> which it must turn over to the next generation increased, and not
> impaired, in value.
>
> Theodore Roosevelt, 1907

This is a book with many purposes. First, it is a book about wetland regulation, and the impact of changing from federal to state preeminence in the administration of wetland resources. As we explain in the initial chapters of this book, wetlands are a critical environmental resource that contribute to the sustainability of several species while also contributing to the quality of human life. There is no doubt that protecting wetlands is an important priority for both the federal and state governments. There is, however, substantial disagreement between the states and federal agencies regarding both the scope of wetland protection and the implementation of existing policy. Many states, industries, and environmental protection groups are dissatisfied with the current implementation of wetland protection through section 404 of the Clean Water Act. This dissatisfaction has led a number of states to examine the possible formal assumption of federal authority to regulate wetlands. What is uncertain is: (1) what level of government will take the lead in regulating this resource; (2) how that authority, which currently resides in the federal government, can be devolved back to the states while also maintaining federal standards; and (3) whether assumption can in fact rectify the concerns of the states, interest groups, and industries that are affected by wetland regulation. We address each of these questions in this volume.

On another level this is a book about federalism and intergovernmental relations. The debate over the respective roles of the federal and state governments in the regulation of environmental resources has led to the emergence of a growing body of literature addressing what is commonly termed "environmental federalism." In our study of section 404 assumption, we examine a policy alternative that, when implemented, transfers primary authority for regulating a vital resource from the national government to the states. However, the delegation of regulatory authority is subject to a variety of constraints that find their roots in the fundamental divisions between state and national authority in our Constitution.

On yet another level, this is a study about program implementation, that important yet still amorphous area of policy science that is of increasing importance as governments confront increasing pressures to enhance programmatic efficiency. There has been an ongoing debate for almost 30 years regarding the definition of implementation, what is implementation success, and how to improve on existing implementation efforts. Improving on the delivery of services through streamlining is one approach to maintaining or increasing government services without an increase in costs. We consider the implementation dimension of state assumption of wetland regulation authority from two perspectives: (1) How state assumption improves on the implementation problems associated with the current national wetland protection program administered under section 404 of the Clean Water Act; and (2) how the implementation literature informs the problems associated with the *process* of assumption by the states. To date, two states have assumed full authority for section 404—Michigan and New Jersey—while almost 20 have deigned to pass on assumption of federal authority.

In this volume, we examine the state assumption of wetlands permitting authority as a substantive policy implementation process, as well as a case study of regulatory federalism. In order to present a comprehensive treatment of our subject, we first explain our substantive topic—wetland regulation—and present a theoretic framework for considering section 404 assumption by states. Chapter 1 discusses the problem of wetland regulation, and initially introduces the alternative to federal wetland regulation: the state assumption of federal authority. Then, the concept of environmental federalism is discussed, and the implementation approach to assessing the environmental federalism problem is introduced. The chapter ends with a discussion of the methods used to conduct the study of section 404 assumption.

Chapter 2 provides an overview of the environmental and economic functions, and presents a brief history of wetlands in the United States. The importance of wetlands as ecosystems is discussed, and the benefits derived from wetlands are identified. Methods of wetlands degradation are identified. We also describe the regulation of wetlands prior to the Clean Water Act, including both the legislative history and judicial precedent that helped establish the authority of the federal government to regulate activities in private property.

Chapter 2 offers grounding in the scientific and institutional context and creates a substantive backdrop for chapter 3, which summarizes the development of the current federal wetlands regulation program under the Clean Water Act. Chapter 3 identifies the deficiencies and advantages of wetlands regulation as well as the recurring problems associated with implementation of federal wetlands regulation. Alternatives to the existing wetlands regulatory regime are also discussed, with an emphasis on the statewide wetlands plans that are based on state assumption of the federal program. The state assumption process is outlined and discussed, and the methodology used to examine state perspectives and experiences with assumption is introduced.

In chapter 4, we examine the Michigan and New Jersey experiences in assuming section 404 from the EPA. These two cases indicate that assumption was a difficult process for each state. Two states considering section 404 assumption in the mid-1990s, Maryland and Florida, are examined in chapter 5. The Maryland Department of Environmental Protection, despite recent rejection of assumption legislation, is moving ahead with plans to assume 404. Florida has deferred assumption for several years, because of a variety of potential problems involving reconciliation of federal and state wetlands policy, as well as dynamic political change in the state legislature.

In chapter 6, we turn to consider a selection of those states that opted to forego section 404 assumption. Although these states have a variety of wetlands resources and differing state-level regulatory regimes, each has rejected assumption for similar reasons. Then, in chapter 7, we discuss the lessons to be learned about wetlands regulation based on the state's experiences with assumption of section 404 responsibilities. The implementation process of 404 assumption is discussed in the context of the perspectives on implementation advanced in this chapter. And, broader conclusions are advanced about the implementation dimension of environmental federalism.

Although resolution of the problems associated with the regulation of wetlands is beyond the scope of this book, we believe this study helps advance the discussion of state assumption of section 404 in particular, and the regulation of wetland resources in general. On a larger, more theoretic level, it extends the discussion of environmental federalism to consider the implementation problems that will be encountered in efforts to devolve national regulatory authority back to the states. In addition, a careful reflection on the experiences of the diverse array of individuals whose opinions we sought should lend insight into not just why programs succeed or fail, but also to explain why proposed solutions often are foregone due to the structure of decisionmaking in government and the institutionalization of the priorities of stakeholders in the policy process.

This study would not have been possible without the cooperation and assistance of numerous individuals. Our first debt is to the state and federal officials, legislators, journalists, and citizens whose frank, candid answers to our questions about wetland regulation contributed to the depth of this study and made the conduct of the research a real pleasure. Financial support from the endowment of Larry Regens' chair by Freeport-McMoRan Inc., and the Entergy Spatial Analysis Research Laboratory at Tulane University Medical Center was invaluable to the us in the conduct of this study. The University of Oklahoma Research Council and the Carl Albert Center for Congressional Studies provided Keith Gaddie with summer funding and research support to complete the manuscript for publication. Eileen Jones, previously a research assistant to Larry Regens and now on the faculty at Southern University Law School conducted extensive legal research for chapter 2 and drafted text for the cases discussed in that chapter. We are very pleased to share credit for that work with her. Thomas A. Sands and Hadley Wood offered timely and critical comments on early drafts of this study that substantially improved the work.

Substantial thanks are due to series editors Michael Kraft and Harlan Wilson, who made succinct and insightful suggestions on the initial submission. The reviewers at SUNY Press provided helpful advice and comments. Our editors at SUNY Press, Clay Morgan and Zina Lawrence, were especially supportive of this project and very patient in awaiting our final version of the book. As always, this is a collaborative work; the order of the authors is alphabetical, and any errors in the presentation or interpretation of the study are exclusively and equally the property of the authors. As Washington observed, "we must hang together, gentlemen, or most assuredly we will hang separately."

And, finally, we wish to thank our wives and sons for their support and tolerance as we launched ourselves into another round of travel, research, and writing. We love you and want to say that the best part of the research is coming home.

Abbreviations

Acronym	Definition
ADEM	Alabama Department of Environmental Management
ADID	Advanced Identification
CWA	Clean Water Act
CZMA	Coastal Zone Management Area
DOI	U. S. Department of the Interior
EDF	Environmental Defense Fund
EIS	Environmental Impact Statement
EPA	U. S. Environmental Protection Agency
FDEP	Florida Department of Environmental Protection
FDER	Florida Department of Environmental Regulation
FWCPA	Federal Water Pollution Control Act
GAO	U. S. General Accounting Office
KDEP	Kentucky Department of Environmental Protection
MDEP	Michigan Department of Environmental Protection
MdDEP	Maryland Department of Environmental Protection
MOA	Memorandum of Agreement
NEPA	National Environmental Protection Act
NJDER	New Jersey Department of Natural Resources
NMFS	National Marine Fisheries Service
NPDES	National Pollution Discharge Elimination System
NWF	National Wildlife Federation

SCDHEC	South Carolina Department of Health and Environmental Control
SPGP	Statewide Programmatic General Permit
TVA	Tennessee Valley Authority
USACE	U. S. Army Corps of Engineers
USCG	U. S. Coast Guard
USFWS	U. S. Fish and Wildlife Service
WDNR	Wisconsin Department of Environmental Regulation
WMD	Water Management District
WQC	Water Quality Certificat

1

Wetlands, Federalism, and the Implementation Problem

Aided by a little sophistry on the words "general welfare," [the federal branch claim] a right to do not only the acts to effect that which are specifically enumerated and permitted, but whatsoever they shall think or pretend will be for the general welfare.

Thomas Jefferson, 1825

Wetlands policy has become one of the most controversial environmental issues facing the Federal government.

White House Office on Environmental Policy
August 24, 1993

In the wake of the 1994 congressional elections, the regulatory structure of environmental protection as well as the established approach for enforcing environmental laws was brought into question. For the first time in 25 years, serious consideration was given to legislation that would reduce the federal government's preeminence in environmental matters. Virtually the entire framework of environmental legislation enacted since 1970 as well as the federal agencies responsible for environmental management came under scrutiny.

1

One focal point for efforts to limit in federal authority in environmental regulation was in the area of wetland protection. The federal government, acting through the U.S. Environmental Protection Agency (EPA) and the U.S. Army Corps of Engineers (USACE) regulates wetland resources under a component of the Clean Water Act known as section 404. Section 404 started as an effort to improve the quality of water for consumption and human use, reflecting the "swimmable, drinkable" criteria of the original Federal Water Pollution Control Act of 1970. This legislation, especially section 404, has evolved beyond the literal interpretation of navigable waters that it originally regulated, to the point that it is the preeminent policy protecting wetlands.

Critics of section 404 are many and varied, but the criticism from farmers, developers, private and property owners is consistent. It was articulated succinctly by the Kentucky Farm Bureau's director of National Affairs and Political Education, who stated that section 404 was "a pervasive and restrictive land-use policy affecting primarily private landowners" (Cansler, 1997). Reducing the federal government's authority to protect wetlands has now become a controversial component of the larger movement to redesign the nation's environmental regulatory regime. The most recent effort, HR 961, was designed to address many of the concerns of critics. When introduced and debated in 1995, it passed the House 240-185, but no action was taken in the Senate. Subsequent sessions of Congress have failed to produce any changes. As a result, in the controversy over regulating wetlands the debate returns to another alternative for addressing particular concerns of the regulated public: state assumption of federal regulatory authority over section 404.

The concept that federal authority should devolve to the states is neither new nor novel in the American regulatory experience. Major components of the Clean Water Act, especially sections 101, 310, and 401, have been delegated. Hazardous waste policy established by the Resource Conservation and Recovery Act (RCRA) has been delegated, devolving to 44 states as of 1991. Indeed, the evolution of the EPA since the 1970s has led to a dramatic increase in indirect regulation—the use of state and federal agencies to enact federal mandates, with the EPA serving as coordinating agency for the myriad actors involved in environmental protection.

For over two decades the U.S. Environmental Protection Agency (EPA) has encouraged states to assume authority for the federal discharge-and-fill permit program under section 404 of the Clean Water Act. This section of the Clean Water Act is one of the most extensive in terms of its impact on land-use; combined with section 10 of the

Rivers and Harbors Act it serves as the principal vehicle at the national level for protecting wetlands. The effort to encourage state assumption of section 404 is purportedly designed to reduce the repetitive nature of the wetlands regulation process. However, it has not met with the success of RCRA delegation, or the delegation of other parts of the Clean Water Act, which 38 states have assumed. Only two states have successfully assumed the section 404 program. State water resource regulators have offered a variety of reasons for not assuming the federal program, citing a variety of factors ranging from limits on administrative autonomy to political constraints to the costs of assuming the program from the federal government.

The arguments offered by state regulators for not pursuing assumption of a major program like section 404 take on added relevance if the federal role in wetlands protection is diminished. The dynamics of section 404 assumption and the problems noted by state and federal agencies illustrate the broader issues encountered in a general shift toward greater reliance on the states for regulatory enforcement.

State assumption is an option that has a great deal of support across many constituencies. The World Wildlife Fund (1992) suggested that statewide comprehensive wetlands permitting offers enormous potential for addressing the current controversies in wetland protection. The National Wetlands Policy Forum recommended state assumption as being the best approach for assuring no-net-loss of wetlands. State assumption of the federal section 404 discharge-and-fill permitting program is a central feature of such wetlands strategies. The 404 program—administered by the U.S. Army Corps of Engineers (USACE) on behalf of the Environmental Protection Agency—is at the center of the wetlands regulation controversy which we discuss at length in chapter 3. The areas of concern for the states regarding federal administration of section 404 may not be addressed by the assumption option. This factor in particular caused us to question if assumption really is the best course of action for states seeking to protect wetlands.

The actions of states after their initial examination of the assumption option indicates that there are substantial drawbacks for the states. Before 1989, only Michigan had assumed section 404 authority. Subsequently, New Jersey completed assumption in 1993 and Maryland was moving forward with the assumption process as late as 1996. On the other hand, 20 states explored and rejected assumption of the federal program. By examining the factors inducing states to accept or reject assumption, it is possible to identify what is in store for states which seek and then obtain section 404 authority from the EPA; what aspects of the program make assumption unattractive to the states; and what insights can be gleaned from the 404 experience for designing and implementing a system of regulatory federalism that encourages state assumption of federal authority.

Federalism and the Implementation Problem

Part of the controversy that surrounds environmental regulation arises from fundamental assumptions in the American constitutional design. The structure of American federalism is determined by the constitutional relationship between the national and state governments. The federal structure of the governments in the United States presumes the preeminence of the national government through the supremacy clause, and subsequent court decisions have repeatedly affirmed this supremacy (Nice and Fredericksen, 1994). However, certain powers are reserved to the states.

The division of governmental authority between the national and state governments often creates situations in which the national government wants to enact a comprehensive national policy, but must act through the states, either due to the constitutional restrictions on direct national government action, or because practical limitations on resources or personnel available to the national agencies means coordination or cooptation through a state agency is more expedient. The problems associated with state/federal coordination within policy areas have created the area of study known as regulatory federalism.

The concept of regulatory federalism is relevant to discussions of state assumption of section 404 of the Clean Water Act. Regulatory federalism is not a new concept in the American experience, although it has only been a broad political concern since the emergence of extensive social legislation in the New Deal. Under regulatory federalism, the policy imperatives of the national government are implemented in coordination with, or directly through, state and local agencies. At the present time, the problems and conflicts of state/federal relations are most apparent in the area of environmental regulation because state and local governments confront the potential for major shifts in responsibilities for environmental management (Wise and O'Leary, 1997).

Despite the preeminence of the national government, disputes regarding the design and implementation of public policy have constantly emerged in advance of the national government's movement into controversial social policies such as civil rights and environmental protection. As early as the New Deal, the national government used the funding of roads to compel bureaucratic reforms of state agencies (Anderson, 1973). A noted example of resistence at the time to such efforts was observed in Georgia in 1935, where a generous grant of $10 million for road construction was contingent on the fulfilment by the state's governor of an agreement to reform the state department of transportation. There was not a dispute over the reform of the department; however, federal officials attempted to control the implementation of reform and the targeting of granted funds, which hindered both reform and implementation of new construction. Environmental scholars often observe the same problem in modern *environmental federalism*, where, as Wise and O'Leary observe, "federal, state, and local agencies are sometimes partners and sometimes protagonists" (1997: 152).

The current design of federal regulation reflects that earlier dispute, by requiring that the states be in compliance with federal regulations when assuming responsibility for the implementation of federal programs. In the case of the Clean Water Act's section 404, this means that state assumption will necessarily lead to the enforcement of a delineation standard (the application of definitive criteria for identifying wetlands) and regulatory standards for the protection of wetlands (i.e., allowable development activities in wetlands) that are at least as rigorous as existing federal standards. It follows that, in the context of regulatory federalism, the assumption of federal authority may not carry the benefits that one would expect. Although the actual implementation of regulation has been transferred to the state, the ability of the states to modify the regulatory regime is dramatically curtailed.

Environmental Federalism

The environmental federalism debate can be effectively divided into two "generations" of thought. The first generation, which was advanced in the 1960s, was characterized by strong, centralized national regulation. The second generation emerged in the 1980s and calls into question the approach of the first generation. Instead, second-generation scholarship advocates a more flexible, decentralized approach (Esty, 1996). This debate usually focuses on questions of goal-based versus prescriptive regulation, and indirectly on fundamental issues of constitutional preeminence.

A brief history of environmental regulation reveals that the national government's concern with the regulation of natural resources has a long history, while public health concerns have largely been left to local communities and the states. Some states and localities enacted air and water pollution laws in the early part of the twentieth century, but the states did not actively move to address environmental problems in a systematic fashion until the 1950s. Federal programs at that time were largely designed to support state efforts such as the creation of water treatment facilities which we discuss in chapter 2. Environmental regulation was largely limited in scope, a product of state initiative to either finance regulation or seek federal grants, and was quite variable from state to state (Rabe, 1986).

Increased concern with environmental quality emerged in the 1960s, due to a variety of catalysts. Certainly the most famous, the publication of Rachel Carson's book *Silent Spring* (1962), focused attention on potential threats to human health and created increased demand for environmental protection. A number of states responded by reorganizing or streamlining their existing programs to make them more effective, such as happened in Minnesota with the creation of its Pollution Control Agency, or by creating new agencies to focus on pollution control as happened in Illinois (see Switzer, 1993).

Ironically, it has been argued that the growth of the states' attention to environmental matters led business to demand *an increased federal presence*. In particular, according to Samuel Hays (1985), business and industry interests sought to have the federal government preempt state authority and thereby limit the impact of differential state regulation. In less than a decade, efforts to expand federal regulation of the environment, especially the passage of two major pieces of legislation—the Clean Air Act (1970) and the Federal Water Pollution Control act (1972)—altered the federal/state balance in environmental regulations. This trend was reinforced by other environmental legislation which soon followed, including the Safe Drinking Water Act (1974), the Resource Conservation and Recovery Act (RCRA, 1976), and the Comprehensive Environmental Response, Compensation, and Liability Act (CERCLA or "Superfund," 1980). In part this legislation was beneficial to business, because it created unified national standards, and it also attained the preemption goal discussed above (c.f. Elliott, *et al.*, 1985; Rose-Ackerman, 1981). And, as Daniel C. Esty noted in a recent piece in the *Michigan Law Review* (1996), presidential politics may have played a role in ensuring passage of the Clean Air Act. One of President Richard Nixon's potential challengers in 1972 was the strongly pro-environmental senator from Maine, Edmund Muskie.

The next era of environmental federalism coincided with the election of Ronald Reagan as president. Reagan's campaign to "turn government back to the people"—the states and localities—included efforts to return environmental regulation to the states. And within the academic literature on federalism there was a resurgence of the argument for federalism as a "laboratory" for policy experimentation, and of other concepts such as competitive federalism—the idea that localities should be able to compete for residents, investment, and business based on the ability to provide variable forms of government and regulation that stand in contrast to each other (Dye, 1990). This argument—that people "will vote regulation with their feet"—parallels many of the initial concerns that promoted strong federal intervention in the environment. That is, the assumption that localities will "bid down" in order to attract investment and residents, and as a consequence create potential externalities, such as pollution, that will spillover into other communities (see also Nice and Frederickson, 1994). This debate has now come full circle, with many business and industry groups demanding a return of authority to the states in order to get out from under the more onerous aspects of national environmental regulations (Switzer, 1993).

The renewed debate over environmental federalism is related to the evolution of the mission of the Environmental Protection Agency (see Wise and O'Leary, 1997; Manley, 1987). At the outset of the agency's existence, the EPA was a hands-on agency with a high degree of centralization. As Lewis Crampton observed in the *EPA Journal*, "In 1970 the EPA wrote the regulations, set the standards, issued the permits, and did most of the monitoring, inspection, and enforcement work involved in ensuring compliance with national environmental rules" (1984: 4). Within 15 years EPA had responded to congressional imperatives for an increased state and local role in regulation and enforcement. The EPA evolved into "the primary operational arm of a *network for environmental protection*" (Crampton, 1984: 5; emphasis added). Manley (1987) extends this observation, arguing that the decentralization advocated in Ronald Reagan's version of New Federalism emerged as the prevailing view in environmental regulation.

A consequence of the devolvement of federal authority to regulate the environment to the states is the emergence of environmental federalism as an area of study (see Lester, 1994; Ringquist, 1993). However, the areas of concern for environmental federalism are not at all new. James P. Lester (1994) has observed that while the study of environmental federalism is a relatively new endeavor, the need to focus on environmental policy below the federal level is not. Paul Sabatier (1973) lamented the lack of sub-national studies of environmental policymaking over a decade before the initial cry for a return to states as the principal actor in environmental regulation. At the time, Sabatier argued that such an examination would probably reveal "considerable variance in the implementation of federal standards from state to state." So, despite the existence of a federal mandate and explicit baseline standards in many areas of environmental regulation, state-level implementation and compliance was not likely to be consistent. Subsequent to Sabatier's lament, a flurry of quantitative and qualitative studies of state environmental policymaking have been produced. Lester (1994) noted that no fewer than 25 published studies, focusing mainly on hazardous waste policy and the consequences of what became termed environmental federalism, exist. And, in large part these studies are concerned with problems of implementation: how federal programs are implemented, why implementation varies despite uniform standards, whether increased state authority and autonomy can improve the delivery of regulation and the attainment of policy goals.

With regard to our particular area of concern—the assumption by states of Clean Water Act section 404 authority—there has been ample opportunity for states to take over this program. The EPA has actively promoted state assumption of federal authority since the 1970s, placing this program at the forefront of the movement away from the use of highly centralized national agency in environmental regulation. Despite the apparent opportunity to bring implementation of environmental regulation closer to the regulated public, there has been little effort to assume section 404. Our analysis demonstrates that section 404 has remained largely out of state hands due to a variety of problems with both the program and the process of assumption that are related to implementation. Further, those problems will likely constrtain future efforts to devolve federal regulatory authority back to the states.

Implementation and Federalism

Before proceeding with our evaluation of the state assumption problem, it is important to delineate our underlying theoretical framework. Implementation of the section 404 program has grown in controversy over the two decades of its existence, and that controversy is at the heart of initial state efforts to assume the program. The problems with 404 also raise process implementation questions. In our examination of section 404 and state assumption, we are concerned primarily with the mechanism for assumption, what policymakers believe assumption can or will do, and why the active pursuit of a key component of the Clean Water Act—the assumption by the states of section 404 authority—has encountered resistance. Resistance to the delegation of state authority raises several questions regarding the wetlands permitting system and the implementation of assumption of that system by the states:

1. *How was the assumption process implemented?* As we will observe in the course of this study, one of the barriers to assumption of wetlands protection has been the perception that implementing the assumption process is difficult. The process is viewed as time-consuming, onerous, and laden with administrative and political pitfalls.

2. *What are the goals of states in seeking assumption?* It is fashionable in modern social science to characterize decisionmaking in terms of costs and benefits (Rhoads, 1985). If costs and benefits structure policy decisions, we should expect that if a state has goals it seeks that can be attained through the assumption of the 404 program, then the net benefits of assumption will be positive. If, however, the costs associated with the assumption of federal authority outweigh the potential benefits, assumption loses its appeal.

3. *Will section 404 assumption help states obtain those goals?* It is possible that state goals are not attained through assumption. Indeed, assumption may prove to hinder rather than enhance attainment of goals. If so, the choice of assumption will not be attractive because the goals of state policymakers do not exist in the realm of possible outcomes that exist under an assumed program.

An overview of the implementation literature helps frame our analysis, especially to enhance understanding of why performance often did not meet promise. The study of implementation has emerged since the early 1970s. The initial generation of policy implementation studies focused on understanding how an authoritative decision was executed by the bureaucracy. These analyses—typified by Pressman and Wildavsky's classic study of initial work on neighborhood development programs in Oakland, California (1973)—were case-oriented, and often detailed the complex nature of a particular program's implementation, often in a particular locality. This research initially identified the coordination and control problems that have been endemic to subsequent studies of implementation. These studies initially identified a variety of factors that explained the typical failure of programs to meet expectations.

Critics of the initial generation of implementation studies leveled two important criticisms. The first is subjective: Initial studies focused on policy failures, and couched their findings in terms of "why things didn't work." The initial second generation of research seemed to focus on refuting Pressman and Wildavsky's depressing declaration of how "great expectations in Washington are dashed in Oakland." The second criticism of first-generation research is centered on methodological concerns. The case-oriented approach underlying first-generation studies is often criticized for its lack of a theoretical basis, and for suffering from what became the classic "too few cases, too many variables" problem. In other words, how could one make generalizations about implementation based on case studies that may be unique? In the process of addressing these concerns, the study of implementation divided loosely into two camps, based on the framing and study of the implementation question: the top-down versus the bottom-up orientation.

The top-down perspective approached implementation as a search for key variables to help explain when implementation succeeds or fails. Advocates of this perspective argue that policy flows from principles at the senior levels of government. Evaluating implementation success becomes an exercise in how or whether those senior-level priorities are applied at lower levels, and then ascertaining the conditions that promote or discourage compliant implementation. Paul Sabatier (1983) neatly summarized the theoretical perspective and goals of a top-down approach to implementation study in a series of four questions:

1. To what extent were the actions of implementing officials and target groups consistent with the objectives and procedures outlined in the policy decision?

2. To what extent were the objectives attained over time, that is, to what extent were the impacts consistent with the objectives?

3. What were the principal factors affecting policy outputs and impacts, both those relevant to the official policy as well as other politically significant ones?

4. How was the policy reformulated over time on the basis of experience?

Implementation success is then measured as the degree to which policy goals, set by top-level formulators, are translated into policy outcomes. What, then, are the key factors that structure implementation?

Since the initial implementation studies of the early 1970s, a growing body of research has reached similar conclusions regarding the significant variables affecting implementation success from the top down. Sabatier and Mazmanian (1980, 1979) were the first scholars to systematically identify what Sabatier (1980) had termed the "legal, political, and tractability variables" that affect implementation. Collectively, other scholars, including Van Meter and Van Horne (1975) Van Horne and Van Meter (1976), and Ripley and Franklin (1982) have identified no fewer than ten different variables that affect implementation success from the top down. The most coherent and theoretically sound articulation of these variables comes from Sabatier (1980), who identifies six broadly defined variables, which, according to Mazmanian and Sabatier (1983), served as the basis of 21 separate studies in the 1970s and 1980s. Those variables, and elaborations on the importance of each, are:

1. Clear and Consistent Objectives. Stated simply, are the goals of the policy clearly articulated and not internally conflicting? Clear goals and unambiguous procedures that avoid goal conflict also serve to enhance implementation success.

2. Adequate causal theory. Will the policy levers and jurisdiction of the implementors be adequate to affect change? Or, is the theory that underlies the program flawed, and therefore a potential impediment to implementation success?

3. Implementation processes are legally structured to enhance compliance by implementing officials and target groups. This variable in particular is broadly structured, and incorporates what Sabatier (1983) termed "a variety of legal mechanisms including the veto points involved in program delivery, the sanctions and incentives available to overcome resistance, and the assignment of programs to implementing agencies which would be supportive and give [the policy program] a high priority" (23). Some research has treated each legal dimension as a separate variable (see Bullock and Lamb, 1985).

4. Committed and skillful implementing officials. Do the people who are tasked the job want the job? Lipsky (1971) noted in one of his bottom-up studies of the urban reform that implementor commitment and skills enhanced implementation success. Statutes have occasionally placed programs explicitly in the hands of committed officials (the Civil Rights Act of 1964, or the Endangered Species Act), but often these decisions are the product of "post-statutory political forces" (Sabatier, 1983: 23).

5. Support of Interest Groups and Soveriegns. Given the length of time required for successful implementation (Sabatier, 1983), continued support from powerful political entities is important for a policy's implementation and reformulation. There is extensive empirical evidence, especially in environmental policymaking, that the support or opposition of efforts to expand or reform Clean Air regulation by congressional leaders and the executive often enabled or frustrated, respectively, the ability to successfully formulate and implement policy (Regens, 1989).

6. Changes in socioeconomic conditions which do not substantially undermine political support or causal theory. Policies do not exist in static space, but rather they move through time. And, the conditions of space change over time This can affect the relevance and appropriateness and therefore the adequacy of the causal theory (condition 2), or political support for the program. An excellent example comes from our particular area of interest in this study, wetland protection. The support for wetland regulation in the eastern United States has been subject to some waning with the rightward political shift of the United States in the 1980s. As the implementation of the section 404 program was perceived to become more intrusive on small landowners, southern politicians who had previously supported water regulation (Billy Tauzin, R-LA, for example) became more critical of federal implementation of the section 404 discharge and fill program.

These six broad variables identified three conditions that precede implementation in the design phase of the policy process, and three that can affect policy over time and therefore are matters of importance to reformulation. The focus of the top-down scholar, then, is on how political and policy factors hindered or helped implementation, to what extent field-level implementors and targets of policy complied with top-level goals and procedures, and whether experience contributed to modification or improvement of the implementation process.

In contrast the "bottom-up" approach assumes that the problem of understanding implementation flows from the lack of meaningful feedback between the individuals who understand problems—field-level implementors—and the initial set of policy formulators (Hjern 1982; Lipsky, 1978). In particular, the bottom-up perspective is critical of other second-generation studies precisely because of their focus on compliance with top-level directives in an hierarchical organization. Further, in the absence of Sabatier's first three conditions, the predictive power of top-down models was suspect at best. Instead, to understand implementation, the bottom-up approach argues that scholarship should focus on the strategic initiatives from "street-level" implementors and other policy subsystems that are relevant to the target (see Prottas, 1979). Doing so would allow for the construction of implementations structures that tracked backwards from "solving" the problem.

The lack of predictive power of the Sabatier model was also of importance to bottom-up critics of the top-down approach, especially in the absence of the first three variables identified by Sabatier. The top-down perspective structures the policy process to respond to the perceptions of the field-level implementor, not unlike backward mapping. Sabatier (1983) and Goggin, Bowman, Lester, and O'Toole (1990) observed that criticisms by the bottom-up implementation perspective—especially the information feedback and emphasis by top-down scholars on hierarchies—were largely valid. But, these scholars also assert that such a bottom-driven implementation approach has serious, detrimental consequences for democratic representation and political accountability.

Goggin and his colleagues also observe that, on a more positive note, this generation of research produced analytic frameworks that suggest implementation depends on three broad sets of factors that facilitate the creation of an incorporated, dynamic model of the implementation process: policy form and content; the structure of organizations and/or policy systems and their resources; and the motivations and communications among people involved in implementation. In particular, these studies establish that implementation will vary over time or among constituencies, and is subject to alteration and reformulation. The role of history and context was brought to the fore of understanding "how things work."

Much like the initial first-generation studies, the second-generation studies suffered from a lack of generalizeability, leading some implementation scholars to encourage the development of a "third-generation" perspective. This perspective returns to Rose's (1973) observation that states as unique actors can have varying levels of success in implementing policy. In an effort to move toward a third-generation approach to implementation, Goggin and his colleagues (1990) incorporated the variability of state capacity to implement into a dynamic model that considers feedback and changes in policy over time to reflect implementation success. Their approach assumes that communication in the policy process flows both up and down in the implementation process, thereby incorporating the best elements of the bottom-up approach to implementation—localized innovations and feedback in the policy process—and the legal responsibility and legitimating aspects of hierarchical control from the top-down model into a dynamic system.

Our study considers three aspects of implementation as it relates to assumption by the states of the federal permitting program. First, are the end goals of states that consider assumption consistent with the outputs and design of an assumed program? Second, how does the assumption process facilitate, impede, or discourage state assumption of the program? And finally, throughout this work and especially in the final chapter, we assess the prospects for implementation success or failure of the assumption process from the three principal perspectives discussed in the previous section: top-down, bottom-up, and in a dynamic communications model. In essence, we seek to understand the dynamic behind changing the implementation process, given the potential transformation of the environmental regulatory regime in the United States. If the interaction between the states and the federal government under the 404 permitting experience is any indication, protracted negotiation regarding state program design and the balance of authority between states and federal agencies is likely to occur.

Method, Data, and Sources

In discussing the problems associated with section 404 assumption, we have paid careful attention, when appropriate, to the concerns of the third-generation implementation scholars. Yet we also go "back to the future" in method; we employ a paired-comparison, case-study approach. This allows us to examine the assumption experience of pairs of states at similar stages in the assumption process, especially the role of state capacity and federal financial support. We then broaden our scope to examine states that are not pursuing assumption in order to understand their viewpoints about the problems associated with the process. Unlike the dominant emphasis of implementation scholars, who are concerned with supporting a prevalent paradigm, we use the perspectives offered by their research to understand the problems associated with state assumption of federal authority under the Clean Water Act.

Recent studies of both environmental federalism (Ringquist, 1993) and implementation (Goggin, et al., 1990) relied on quantitative, 50-state comparisons of programs to model federal relations. When appropriate, we are both strong advocates of rigorous quantitative approaches. However, in this study because it is more appropriate, we opted to rely heavily on narratives—interviews, legislation, court cases, and document analysis—to study the implementation problem in state-federal wetland regulation in order to obtain an in-depth understanding. This use of comparative cases allows us to use the depth of information available to support conclusions about state-federal regulation. Therefore, we have endeavored to craft a comprehensive collection of elite interviews, paired with scientific, legal, and policy history to answer the questions advanced in this chapter.

In order to assess the 404 assumption experience of states, we have relied on a variety of primary and secondary sources. State implementors of section 404 activities in Florida, Michigan, Maryland, Nebraska, New Jersey, and Wisconsin were interviewed initially by telephone. Then, face-to-face interviews with administrative and implementing personnel were conducted in Florida, Michigan, and New Jersey. The interviews with key state officials were supplemented with a series of telephone interviews of selected Corps of Engineers and EPA officials. The viewpoints of state legislators and staff members of relevant oversight committees in Florida, Michigan, and New Jersey were also obtained through correspondence, telephone, and in-person contacts. In all, 26 interviews were conducted either over the phone or in person with state and federal officials who are relevant to the cases.

In addition to interview data, the states included in this study generously provided copies of written background materials on their state wetlands protection program, including feasibility studies, and state assumption applications that were submitted to the EPA. The feasibility study for Michigan was supplemented by published evaluations of that state's 404 program (see Bostwick, 1989). We also relied on previous EPA analyses of state assumption and the performance of the 404 program. In addition, we obtained state feasibility studies from eight states that considered and ultimately rejected assumption of 404 authority: Alabama, Kentucky, Nebraska, Minnesota, North Carolina, Oregon, South Carolina, and Wisconsin. Telephone interviews with state permitting officials in those states were conducted to supplement our analysis of the findings we noted in the feasibility studies.

Telephone and face-to-face interviews were conducted using an open-ended, informally structured interview technique. While all interview points were covered by all respondents, we permitted respondents to direct the interview into a variety of related topic areas that ultimately contributed to the depth of our analysis. All interview respondents were assured of anonymity at the time of the interviews, and their names are therefore withheld in this study. We are convinced that strict anonymity prompted more ready and frank responses than would have resulted from "on-the-record" interviews. The politically sensitive nature of many of these state regulatory environments reinforces our maintenance of anonymity.

Systematically evaluating state assumption of consolidated permitting authority for wetlands development necessitated reliance primarily on qualitative rather than quantitative techniques. Where possible, we have supplemented our largely qualitative interview information with other empirical evidence to support our findings and conclusions. The two cases of successful state assumption provide a baseline for understanding how the assumption of federal programs by state agencies may proceed. Starting from this baseline, it is possible to identify the potential pitfalls awaiting the states that attempt 404 assumption. Because of the in-depth nature of our analysis, the multi-actor nature of the implementation of 404— which involves four federal agencies and at least one or more state agency—offers broad insights into the problems facing states in assuming responsibility for federal programs, especially when federal interagency disputes arise.

2

Wetlands in the United States

The greatest domestic problem facing our country is saving our soil and water; our soil belongs also to unborn generations.

Sam Rayburn, 1956

What if we say that if it is wet, it's a wetland?

Dan Quayle, 1989

The wetland issue has assumed a prominent position on the U.S. environmental agenda. Historically perceived as useless wastelands or swamps, wetlands are increasingly recognized in the last quarter of the twentieth century as an important natural resource. The decline of wetlands is readily apparent as sportsmen and trappers note dwindling numbers of wildlife and fish, flooding increased along rivers and shorelines, and water quality declining (Meeks and Runyon, 1990). At the same time, scientific research continues to identify a variety of environmental and economic roles filled by the wetland. Yet, despite the economic value of wetlands for flood control, water purification, recreational facilities, and species habitats as well as their aesthetic value, no comprehensive federal legislation governs the use and preservation of wetlands.

As is typical with emerging policy issues, substantial controversy has accompanied the development of wetlands regulation in the United States. The current federal wetlands protection program is under constant criticism from builders and private land owners for being unduly onerous, while environmentalists complain that those same regulations are inadequate to protect wetlands resources. Cansler (1997) and the National Wetlands Forum (1990) provide examples of these competing criticisms.

What Are Wetlands?

The definition of wetlands is broader than the general public might expect. Beyond the usual swamps, marshes, and bogs that come to mind when one mentions wetlands, areas which are governed by wetlands regulation also include woody areas which sustain wetlands vegetation, dry desert furrows, formerly marshy meadowlands, occasionally saturated lands, and arctic tundra (Alaska has 170 million acres of U.S. wetlands). The U.S. Environmental Protection Agency (EPA) defines wetlands as:

> Those areas that are inundated or saturated by surface or ground water at a frequency to support, and under normal circumstances do support, a prevalence of vegetation typically adapted for life in saturated soil conditions. Wetlands generally include swamps, marshes, bogs, and similar areas (33 CFR Section 328.3(b) [1989]).

A more entertaining definition came from the observations of a Kentucky farmer who said they were lands "too wet to plough and too

Figure 2-1: Types of Wetlands

Swamp	Wetland dominated by trees or shrubs.
Marsh	A frequently or continually inundated wetland characterized by vegetation adapted to saturated soil conditions.
Bog	A peat-accumulating wetland that has no significant inflows or outflows and supports mosses, particularly sphagnum.

(continued)

Figure 2-1: (Continued)

Fen	A peat-accumulating wetland that receives some drainage from surrounding mineral soil and visually supports marsh-like vegetation.
Peatland	A generic term for any wetland that accumulates partially decaying plant matter.
Muskeg	Large expanses of peatlands or bogs; commonly used term in Canada and Alaska.
Bottomland	Lowlands along streams and rivers, usually on alluvial floodplains that are periodically flooded. Bottomlands are often forested and sometimes called bottomland hardwood forests. The Okeefenokee Swamp in Georgia and the Atchafalaya in Louisiana are examples. Bottomlands provide shelter and food for deer, wildcat, cougar, fox, raccoon, beaver, muskrat, quail, dove, duck and a variety of reptiles.
Wet Prairie	Similar to marsh.
Wet Meadow	Grassland with waterlogged soil near the surface but without standing water for most of the year. Located along streams and lakes in poorly drained low-lying areas. Provide food and habitat for small birds, mammals, and reptiles.
Slough	A swamp or shallow lake system in the northern and midwestern U.S. or slowly flowing shallow swamp or marsh in the southeastern U.S.
Pothole	Shallow, marsh like pond formed by ancient glaciers. Found primarily in the Great Plains states of Montana, North and South Dakota, and western Minnesota. Potholes produce approximately 50 percent of the annual duck hatch and provide homes to about 7 million breeding ducks.
Playa	Marsh like pond similar to pothole, but with different geological origin (southwest U.S.).
Tundra	Treeless, freshwater marsh covered by sedges and cotton grass only found in Alaska. Occurs in low-lying lands in northern and western Alaska where ground beneath the surface is permanently frozen (permafrost). Water birds and shore birds are common, as are migratory fowl that nest here. Caribou herds, grizzly bear, wolf, moose, arctic fox and hare, as well as an occasional polar bear, live on the tundra.

Source: Adapted from Meeks and Runyon (1990)

dry to fish." Wetlands, most broadly defined, are "virtually every piece of ground touched by some form of water" (Miniter, 1991). Because a variety of near-aquatic formations such as sloughs, vernal pools, playas, and prairie potholes also constitute wetlands (See figure 2-1), the simplest definition of a wetland is the transitional areas between open water and dry land. Using this definition, there are approximately 100 million acres of wetlands in the lower 48 states, 90 percent of which are inland wetlands.

Wetlands are always changing. The water that makes a wetland wet may come from ground water, surface water, or direct precipitation. Water presence may change seasonally, which can cause wetlands to appear not to be wet. Because of variation in water supply, the preponderance of vegetation in a wetland will also vary (South Carolina, 1986). Approximately 95 percent of America's wetlands are freshwater wetlands, including a variety of coastal tidal marshes (the seven major classes of wetlands are indicated in figure 2-2).

In 1790, the continental United States contained approximately 221 million acres of wetlands. By 1970, over 50 percent of this total acreage had been destroyed or converted for agricultural or other uses. Most of these losses are in the Mississippi and Ohio River Valleys, the upper Atlantic Coast, and California. According to Dahl (1990, 1991), 22 states have lost over half of their wetlands since the 1790s (see figure 2-3). Of these, six have lost over 80 percent of their wetlands. Despite the commitment of state and federal resources to wetlands protection, approximately 300,000 acres of wetlands are lost every year to regulated activities. From the mid-1970s to the mid-1980s, approximately 2.6 million acres of wetlands were lost. Of the remaining 103.3 million acres of wetlands in 1986, approximately 95 percent were freshwater wetlands (Dahl, 1991).   •

Figure 2-2: Wetlands

COASTAL WETLANDS
Tidal Salt Marshes
    Dominated by the saltwater-tolerant plant species spartina and juncus.
    Plants and animals in these systems are adapted to the stresses of salt-
    water, periodic and regular flooding, and extremes in temperature.
    Over 3.5 million acres along the U.S. coast, especially between southern
    Massachusetts and northern Florida, the Gulf of Mexico, the coast of

(continued)

Figure 2-2: (Continued)

Alaska and isolated areas along the Pacific serve as nursery or spawn-
ing grounds for mullet, flounder, bluefish, menhaden, shrimp, crab, oys-
ters and clams. Geese, duck and other migratory waterfowl live in the
marshes or use them as stops along the migratory flyway.

Tidal Freshwater Marshes

Intermediate on the continuum from coastal salt marshes to freshwater
marshes. They are influenced by tides but without the saltwater stress.

Mangrove Wetlands

Dominated by the red and black mangrove trees. Need protection from
the ocean but exhibit a wide range of saltwater content and tidal influence. Located mostly in southern Florida, (Everglades National Park)
and coastal Louisiana and Texas. Serve as nurseries for shrimp, sea
trout, pompano, tarpon and other fish. Home to such endangered
species as the cougar, crocodile and bald eagle.

INLAND WETLANDS

Freshwater Marshes

Characterized by (1) emergent soft-stemmed aquatic plants such as cat-
tails, pickerelweed, reeds, and several species of grasses and sedges; (2)
a shallow water regime; and (3) generally shallow peat deposits.

Northern Peatlands

Bogs and fens, the two major types of peatlands, occur as thick peat deposits in old lake basins or as blankets across the landscape. Many
formed by the last glacier age, and the peatlands are considered to be a
late stage of a "filling-in" process. Bogs are noted for their nutrient defi-
ciency and waterlogged conditions and for the biological adaptations to
these conditions, such as insect-eating plants (pitcher plants and sun-
dew) and nutrient conservation. Located mainly in northeastern and
north central United States. Provide food and water for moose, deer and
bear.

Southern Deep Water Swamps

Freshwater woody wetlands of the southeastern U.S. that have standing water for most of the growing season. Swamps are normally dominated by cypress, gum, and tupelo trees.

Riparian Wetlands

Found along rivers and streams, these areas are dry for varying portions
of the growing season, being occasionally flooded by nearby water bodies.
Frequently referred to as bottomland hardwood forests, they contain diverse vegetation that varies along with levels of flood frequency.

Source: Adapted from Meeks and Runyon (1990)

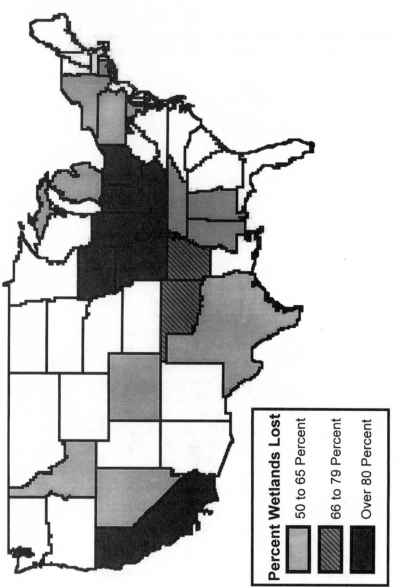

Figure 2-3: Wetland Losses in the United States

Percent Wetlands Lost

- 50 to 65 Percent
- 66 to 79 Percent
- Over 80 Percent

Functions of Wetlands

Wetlands perform a variety of functions, depending on their location, size, and type. Historically thought of as wastelands best suited for fill or dumping, more recent field research reveals that wetlands are among the most productive ecosystems on earth. Because the food productivity of wetlands is especially abundant, wetlands support a variety of animals. Wetlands provide habitat not only for traditional "swamp-dwelling" creatures such as amphibians and reptilians, but also for prairie and forest animals as well as migratory waterfowl such as wild ducks and geese. For example, the decline of migrant duck populations in the Midwest and Plains States is related to the draining and filling of prairie potholes and other isolated wetlands which these ducks used for nesting during their annual migration. Approximately 43 percent of endangered or threatened species in the United States rely in some fashion on wetlands for survival. Over half of all amphibian and fish species currently classified as endangered reside in wetlands (see table 2-1). Wetlands include vast, complicated ecosystems which are crucial to the food chain. Wetlands are important to the production and feeding of fish and shellfish in states such as Louisiana and Florida. Also, a variety of freshwater fish feed in the shallows of wetlands.

Wetlands also provide a variety of functions beneficial to the quality of human life. Wetlands act as natural filtration systems, capable of removing large amounts of sediments, toxins, and nutrients from water runoff. Wetlands vegetation absorbs nutrients which would otherwise enter primary waters, resulting in over-production

Table 2-1. Total Threatened or Endangered Species Associated with Wetlands Habitat in the United States

Species	Percent of Total
Plants	3
Mammals	15
Birds	31
Reptiles	31
Amphibians	50
Fish	57

Source: Mitsch and Gosselink (1986)

of algae and other microbiological organisms which can deplete fish supplies and taint the fresh water supply. Wetlands perform a primary function of controlling pollution through filtration, which protects lakes from accelerated eutrophication—lake aging. Lake aging occurs as lakes become more shallow due to the accumulation of sediment and organic matter. Introducing pollutants further accelerates the aging process. River marshes trap nutrients in plant tissue and impede the buildup of sediment, slowing the aging of lakes.

The most crucial function that wetlands, particularly riparian wetlands, provide for human habitat is flood protection. Wetlands reduce flood peaks by retaining water for a short time and slowing its velocity. For example, Meeks and Runyon (1990) observed that prior to the arrival of Europeans in North America, the Mississippi River bottomland woods stored floodwater equivalent to 60 days of river discharge. As a result, the presence of wetlands substantially reduces the flood risk of dry lands due to river and tributary flooding by slowing the flow of runoff. Wetlands also aid in the recharge of the groundwater supply and serve as repositories for groundwater discharge, thereby helping to regulate stream-flowing, aquifer-dependent areas such as the Great Plains. Ironically, the most common wetlands for this purpose—prairie potholes—have been destroyed by agricultural development in the northern plains, despite the dependence of agriculture in the region on ground water.

Consequences of Wetlands Degradation

There are a variety of consequences of wetlands degradation, many of which result in substantial, though indirect social costs. Species decline and deformity, flooding and its constituent costs, and declining water quality stand out as examples of costs born by the environment and by human society as a consequence of wetland eradication. As we noted above, numerous species rely directly or indirectly on wetlands as habitats for their survival. There are also economic and recreational losses associated with the degradation of wetlands.

The consequences of wetlands degradation for flood control are illustrated by the Great Midwestern Flood of 1993. The Midwest was inundated with rain from throughout the late spring and summer of 1993. As the rains fell, rivers were also fed by melting snows from the heavy winter snowfall in the upper Mississippi Valley. Flooding became a serious problem for many cities on the Mississippi and Missouri River systems. Billions of dollars in damage to croplands and property occurred as a consequence of flooding.

Private and public structures on the Mississippi and Missouri rivers, designed to control flooding and reclaim lowlands for agricultural use, often separated river channels from their natural floodplains and contributed to the flooding in the Mississippi-Missouri Basin. The development and conversion of millions of acres in wetlands to agricultural or commercial use deprived the rivers of natural storage capacity for flood waters. The states hardest-hit by the flood—Missouri, Illinois, and Iowa—also are among the top six states in terms of lost wetlands (see figure 2-3; also Dahl, 1990). The greatest damage was to property in former wetlands, which the swollen rivers reclaimed as floodplains.

Wetlands also serve vital economic and recreational role in the United States. A variety of natural products are obtained from wetlands resources, including furs and fish products. Over 96 percent of the commercial fish and shellfish harvest and over half of the recreational harvest in the United States are dependent on estuary and wetlands systems. Wetlands produce large quantities of wild rice, and are also an important source of timber products. The economic benefits derived from these activities are tremendous. The wetlands-dependent fishing industry alone is worth almost $3.5 billion per year, and the related fish processing industry it supplies was worth almost $27 billion per year in 1990 dollars. Approximately 70 percent of these industries are wetlands dependent.

Water quality, one of the most important goals of environmental regulation, is affected by wetlands degradation. When wetlands absorb runoff, they extract nutrients from the water and deposit them in wetland soil. These nutrients, if allowed to flow unabated into standing waters, lead to algae bloom, which depletes the oxygen content of the water and endangers the resident fish and shellfish populations. When wetlands are allowed to properly function, the deposited nutrients contribute to the rich, fertile soil which supports the variety of wetlands vegetation.

Wetlands Regulation Before Section 404

The evolution of scientific knowledge supporting the economic, social, and ecological value of wetlands has dramatically influenced the federal government's long history of creating policies which impact wetlands. Economic development and public health concerns during the nineteenth and early twentieth centuries led government and private property owners to drain, fill, and pollute millions of acres of swamps, bogs, and flood-plains. Government incentives directly and indirectly led to the draining or filling of isolated wetlands for agricultural use. After World War II, developers filled vast tracts of wetlands in order to facilitate the inexorable housing boom in the suburbs.

The first federal legislation concerned with wetlands was the Swamp Act of 1849. The act authorized Louisiana to drain and fill wetlands for the purpose of reclamation and disease control, and subsequent legislation extended this authority to 12 other states in 1850. This legislation established the groundwork for federal and state policy toward wetlands for the next 100 years. Indeed, until immediately prior to the passage of the federal Water Pollution Control Act of 1970 (FWPCA), Congress was appropriating funds to the Department of Agriculture to fill wetlands (Soil Conservation and Domestic Allotment Act, 16 U.S.C. §590(h), 1968). The national government, through the activities of the U.S. Army Corps of Engineers, destroyed countless acres of wetlands through river diversion and levying projects in the Mississippi and Missouri River Basins. Government programs which encouraged private agricultural expansion through homesteading led settlers to drain and convert numerous other lands. The development of industries that produced large amounts of solid and chemical waste led to the use of these "useless" lands for waste disposal.

Concurrent to funding policies that eradicated wetlands, Congress was also appropriating funds for the then Bureau of Fisheries and Wildlife (now the U.S. Fish and Wildlife Service) to purchase wetlands as preserves for rare and endangered species. In 1934, the Duckstamp program was instituted to develop wetlands refuges for migratory fowl. To date, almost 3.5 million acres of wetlands have been purchased by this levy on hunters licenses. However, the amount of wetlands purchased and preserved is exceeded by the acreage lost to development over the last two decades (Dahl, 1990).

Attitudes toward the destruction of wetlands changed dramatically during the 1960s. Scientific research revealed that wetlands are thriving, vibrant ecosystems which support vital plant and animal life as well as provide a variety of economic and environmental benefits. Mounting empirical evidence in support of wetland preservation emerged at the same time as concerns over first-generation air and water pollution problems were addressed in the late 1960s and early 1970s. In this climate of heightened environmental awareness, federal legislation to protect wetlands resources emerged ancillary to broad water policy legislation, in keeping with the tradition of federal wetlands regulation. In order to better understand current wetlands regulation and the issue of regulatory assumption of wetland protection authority, it is necessary to understand the development of current federal water policy as it relates to wetlands.

Federal Water Quality Legislation

The Refuse Act of 1899 was the first legislation dealing specifically with water pollution. The Act's primary goal was to insure the navigability of the nation's commercial waterways. The problem of water pollution in the late nineteenth century related primarily to the impact of solid waste on the free movement of shipping on inland waterways. Because industry required water for a variety of purposes, most factories and mills were located on or near major waterways. The discharge of solid waste in some areas was so great that the accumulation of waste threatened to choke the physical flow of water—and therefore constituted an obstacle to shipping—on major rivers and their tributaries. The Refuse Act prevented the discharge or deposit of any refuse matter into navigable waters without a permit. Permits were issued by the federal government through the Corps of Engineers, based on the authority retained by the federal government through the Commerce Clause of the Constitution.

It was almost 50 years before new legislation was passed regulating water pollution as a threat to water quality. During this period, the principle issues surrounding water pollution shifted from solid discharges to questions of the quality of water as a consumer resource. In 1948, Congress passed the Water Pollution Control Act, which was designed to encourage water pollution control by state and local governments. The primary means of addressing pollution was authorizing federal research and investigation powers into water pollution, with enforcement left to the states. The 1948 act also authorized the federal government to make loans for water treatment construction, although no appropriation was made to support the program.

Eight years later, the Water Pollution Control Act of 1956 authorized the states to establish water quality standards, using federally sponsored enforcement conferences to negotiate cleanup and compliance. The federal government retained discretionary responsibility of interstate waters. Federal grants were authorized to cover up to 55 percent of construction costs for water treatment. The Water Quality Act of 1965 further extended state authority to set ambient water quality standards, via state-established limits on discharges from individual sources. Although the states retained responsibility for setting standards and enforcement, federal regulators retained oversight authority through approval and enforcement conference procedures similar to those mandated in the Water Pollution Control Act of 1956.

The real beginning of a regulatory presence by the USACE started in the 1960s with the Fish and Wildlife Coordination Act (16 USC Section 662). The act "directed federal agencies involved in the alteration of a water body to consult with the Fish and Wildlife Service with a view to the conservation of wildlife resources" (Want, 1989). The introduction of this statute led the Corps of Engineers to enter a memorandum of agreement with the USFWS. This agreement and the subsequent 1967 regulations formed the basis for the "balancing of competing values" approach used by the USACE in its public interest review.

In 1970, President Nixon allowed the newly established Environmental Protection Agency (EPA) to use the Rivers and Harbors Act (1899) permitting process to regulate pollution discharges into the nation's waters. The passage of the National Environmental Policy Act (NEPA) in 1970 further extended the scope of environment regulation. Section 102 of NEPA requires all federal agencies to issue environmental impact statements (EIS) in connection with taking "major" federal actions "significantly affecting the quality of the human environment." This integration of agency actions in areas of common authority was part of a general effort to bring coherence to environmental policy.

The Clean Water Act

The most significant piece of legislation affecting water quality and the regulation of waterways in the United States was the Federal Water Pollution Control Act of 1972 (FWPCA) and its subsequent amendments, the 1977 Clean Water Act (CWA). The FWPCA set the mission in water quality regulation to "restore and maintain the chemical, physical, and biological integrity of the nation's waters," using the enforcement of technology-based effluent standards on individual dischargers, and limiting the deposition of non-toxic fill and discharges into the waters of the United States.

The EPA was given responsibility for establishing discharge limits and categorizing discharges, and federal agencies also set the terms for issuing and enforcing permits to individual dischargers. States retained the option of assuming a variety of discharge permit programs, provided state standards were at least as stringent as those of the federal government. The Clean Water Act Amendments of 1977 postponed deadlines from the 1972 Act, and clarified the differences between conventional and toxic discharges. The 1977 amendments also expanded the species protection role of the 1972 FWPCA, and clarified the means by which state agencies could assume regulatory authority of the section 404 discharge-and-fill program. Regulations were issued under the act on July 19, 1977.

Section 404

The key component of wetland protection contained in the Clean Water Act is the discharge-and-fill regulations in section 404. Under section 404, the EPA can regulate any discharge into the "waters of the United States," broadly defined. Because of the overlapping jurisdiction of Section 404 and section 10 of the Rivers and Harbors Act of 1899, EPA delegated implementation of section 404 to USACE (the implementing agency for section 10) while retaining an oversight role.

The FWPCA represented a major departure from previous water policy. The term "wetland" is not used in the legislation. Instead, the use of the FWPCA to protect wetlands is derived from judicial decisions that interpret and extend the scope of USACE jurisdiction, largely by expanding the definition of "waters of the United States." The national government took the lead in establishing and regulating national water quality, as well as in issuing and enforcing permits. States assumed a strong role in water quality certification. Under section 401 of the Clean Water Act, the states can block a proposed project by refusing to grant a water quality certificate. States can further expand their role in the regulation of water quality and water use by assuming authority for other sections of the Clean Water Act from the EPA and Corps, including the section 404 discharge-and-fill program. However, when states assume the program, the federal agencies retain a strong oversight role in evaluating state implementation of water quality protection.

The application of section 404 of the Clean Water Act to the regulation of wetlands has been controversial. Developers, builders, propertyowners, and environmental protection advocates have all agreed at some point that it is reasonable to protect the "swamps, marshes, bogs, and similar areas" indicated in the Fish and Wildlife Service wetlands' definition. The process of identifying and classifying wetlands according to characteristics ascribed to wetlands—delineation—is one of the most contentious problems in the regulation of wetlands. Under the existing regulatory structure that governs wetlands, there has been disagreement between agencies regarding the identification of wetlands. Generally, the Fish and Wildlife Service has been the most liberal in the classification of land as wet, while the Army Corps of Engineers and state agencies have employed less generous methodologies to delineate wetlands. Since 1989, all federal agencies have been required to use the same standard for delineation, although acceptance of the manual that standardized delineation has not been universal. In addition, the variation in delineation of wetlands among the states is still substantial despite the existence of a federal standard. There is substantial controversy regarding the impact of section 404 on lands in the jurisdictional areas that do not provide the wetlands benefits we discussed earlier in this chapter.

Litigation and Court Decisions

As we noted above, the federal government's policy toward use and regulation of wetlands has changed substantially since the beginning of the nineteenth century. Only since the 1870s has the federal government exercised substantial influence in the use and care of the nation's waters. The expansion of federal water powers—which culminated in the 1972 FWPCA and subsequent amendments—has been permitted due to the recent interpretation of the Commerce Clause by the courts. The courts ruled that Congress can regulate the use of a waterway as a disposal under the Commerce Clause, if the waterway is capable of supporting commerce.

Before the 1970s, federal regulation of wetlands was limited by judicial interpretation of the Commerce Clause. Under the Commerce Clause, the federal courts allowed the Corps of Engineers to regulate the condition of "navigable waters." To the extent that a wetland was a navigable water, federal intervention was permissible. However, the definition of navigable waters and the extension of jurisdiction under the commerce clause were taken literally, and federal activity was limited to maintaining the condition of commercial waterways for the purpose of maintaining national economic well-being.

The judiciary gradually broadened the interpretation of navigable waters during the twentieth century. In 1921 the courts ruled the federal government can assert jurisdiction over waterways that had previously been used for commercial transport, regardless of current usage (*Economy Power and Light v. United States*, 256 U.S. 113 [1921]). A 1935 decision upheld a broader test of navigability that expanded federal jurisdiction and established a readily-definable criterion for navigable waters: federal jurisdiction was limited to water above the mean high-water line (*Borax Consolidated v. Los Angeles,* 296 U.S. [1935]). Nonetheless, despite this expansion of the scope of national government power, the vast majority of wetlands continued to lie outside federal regulatory domain.

To fully understand the structure of wetland regulations, it is necessary to add a brief discussion of the case history and legislation that serves as the basis for the Corps of Engineers' participation in section 404, especially through the application of section 10 of the Rivers and Harbors Act (1899). The activist judiciary of the 1960s used the interstate commerce rationale to allow USACE to regulate the dumping of pollutants into federal waters, regardless of the impact on navigation (*United States v. Republic Steel Corporation,* 362 U.S. 482 [1960]; *United States v. Standard Oil Company,* 384 U.S. 224 [1966]). In 1968, USACE was allowed to extend its regulatory mission in navigable waters beyond the maintenance of navigation. In *Zabel v. Tabb* (430 F.2d 199, [1970]), the Court supported the Corps of Engineers authority to consider factors such as conservation, fish and wildlife protection, pollution, aesthetics, ecology, and "the general public interests" when rendering permit decisions. Subsequently, a federal district court ruled that environmental impact statements had to accompany each permit issued by the USACE under the River and Harbors Act (*Kalur v. Tabb,* 335 F. Supp. 1 [1971]). The Court then enjoined the Corps of Engineers from issuing further permits until USACE promulgated regulations which required environmental impact statements. More recently, in relating the role of the commerce clause to section 404, the Supreme Court ruled in *Hodel v. Virginia Surface Mining and Reclamation Association* (452 U.S. 264 [1981]), that "the power conferred by the commerce clause [is] broad enough to permit Congressional regulation of acts causing air or water pollution, or other environmental hazards that may have effects in more that one state" (at 282). At the same time, lower courts supported the denial of permits by the Corps based on the effect of activities on fish and wildlife, although these cases did not factually involve wetlands.

Subsequent to the passage of the FWPCA in 1972, the Corps of Engineers permitting process operated under the same mean-high-water mark test of navigability it had traditionally applied for the preceding 40 years. Under this jurisdictional definition, most wetlands remained outside the purview of federal regulation, and no other federal statute existed which allowed USACE or any other federal agency to address wetlands in a comprehensive fashion.

The federal courts disagreed with the Corps' interpretation of federal jurisdiction vis-a-vis wetlands, and applied a new rationale for federal jurisdiction. Employing geographic analysis of jurisdiction, the courts expanded the federal Commerce Clause power to include most extant wetlands. The courts based their rationale on scientific evidence that water moves in hydrologic patterns, and bodies of water are generally not isolated, but instead are connected as part of aquatic systems. In *Natural Resources Defense Fund v. Callaway* (392 F. Supp. 685 [DD.C. 1975]), the courts ordered the USACE to pass regulations which encompassed wetlands. The Corps of Engineers subsequent ly complied with that order by implementing new rules governing wetlands discharges. A decade later, the Supreme Court reaffirmed the *Callaway* decision in *United States v. Riverside Bayview Homes* (474 U.S. 121 [1985]). The Court's ruling held that USACE's wetlands regulations were constitutional to the extent that the regulations covered wetlands adjacent to navigable-in-fact or potentially navigable waters, or to waters that could plausibly affect interstate commerce.

Summary

Approximately half of all wetlands that existed in the continental United States before 1790 have disappeared. However, a variety of states still have significant tracts of wetlands, and the functions performed by these wetlands contribute to the overall balance of local ecosystems. The variety of wetlands defies a simple definition, which often leads to confusion over the regulation of "wet" resources. Wetlands serve significant roles for human habitation, primarily through flood control, groundwater recharge, and water filtration, and providing habitat to a variety of economically valuable plant and animal species. Wetlands also provide habitat to animal and plant species that are protected by federal and state species control statutes. Although these species do not necessarily have economic value, their intrinsic value has fostered their protection by the government.

Wetlands regulation has emerged in the last quarter-century as a significant and divisive issue on the nation's environmental policy agenda. The statutory history and case law related to wetlands indicates that the precedent for federal involvement in wetlands regulation is well established. At the same time, the importance of wetlands as ecological, economic and aesthetic resources indicate that federal involvement in the management and use of these resources will continue. As a result, current controversies in wetlands regulation surround such questions as: how effectively should the federal government regulate wetlands; should state actors have an expanded role in managing the resource; how can regulation be changed to improve protection of the resource; and can regulation be changed to make it more user-friendly for the regulated public?

Central to answering all of these questions is an understanding of the regulatory environment, especially as it relates to the states. In the next chapter, we describe the existing wetlands regulatory regime. Then, we examine the variety of problems noted by federal resource agencies, the states, and the regulated community with the existing Corps of Engineers implementation of wetlands regulations.

3

Wetlands Protection and Section 404

Whoever fights monsters should see to it that in the process he
doesn't become a monster.

Frederick Wilhelm Nietzsche

There has been a conservation paralysis through regulation.

Corporate officer, Louisiana Land
and Exploration Corporation

I n this chapter, we present an overview of the Clean Water Act's
section 404 program. First, we introduce the legislation and legislative goals that serve as the basis for wetland regulation.
Then, we discuss some of the issues related to the national section
404 program, with an emphasis on the procedural, enforcement, and
consistency of implementation problems, as well as some other substantive "outcomes" issues of concern, such as regulatory takings.
We then provide an overview of specific problems associated with
federal implementation, and discuss the scope and limitations of
state assumption of section 404 authority. This discussion completes
the foundation for our examination of section 404 assumption efforts
that follows in chapters 4 through 6.

Federal Wetland Regulation Authority

Contrary to the perceptions of many casual observers of environmental regulation, no federal legislation is specifically designed to govern the preservation and use of wetlands. Instead, federal regulation of wetlands use is derived from section 404 of the federal Water Pollution Control Act (Clean Water Act) of 1972. The extensive authority to regulate wetland resources, that is granted to EPA through the Clean Water Act, derives from the judicial precedents discussed in the last chapter. Under section 404, it is unlawful for anyone to discharge dredged or fill material into "the navigable waters of the United States," without first receiving permission from the Corps of Engineers. USACE's issuance of a permit is subject to an administrative veto by the EPA, as well as comment and recommendation of a variety of federal agencies, including the USFWS, and in certain regions, the National Marine Fisheries Service (NMFS), the Tennessee Valley Authority (TVA), or the U.S. Coast Guard (USCG) (c.f. O'Toole 1991). Under the Clean Water Act, section 404, the EPA has six established goals:

1. Establish a framework for full implementation of the section 404 discharge-and-fill program;

2. Ensure compliance with the regulations under section 404;

3. Facilitate the transfer of section 404 to the states;

4. Development and implementation of an enforcement program;

5. Development and implementation of programs to foster education and encourage public involvement in the 404 program;

6. Assess and foster research supportive of the mission of section 404.

Current U.S. wetlands policy has been defined by the "no net-loss" criterion established by former President George Bush during his 1988 presidential campaign. The "no-net-loss" policy was developed by Conservation Foundation president William K. Reilly, who went on to become EPA administrator during the Bush administration. Bush moved conspicuously to keep the no-net-loss pledge during his administration (Miniter, 1991). In 1989, new rules governing wetlands conversion were issued which required a permit for any wetland conversion. Previously, the 1986 rules allowed conversion of wetlands less than an acre in size without a permit and conversion of up to 10 acres with USACE permission. The 1986 rules were a product of a 1985 legal settlement negotiated between the Corps of Engineers and the National Wildlife Federation (NWF) (*National Wildlife Federation v. Marsh*, 14 Environmental L. Report. 20262 [DD.C. 1985]). The NWF filed suit to stop efforts by the Ronald Reagan administration, acting through the USACE, from expanding the use of general permits—especially in isolated wetlands—in order to streamline the permit process.

Issues in Wetlands Regulation

The section 404 program is highly controversial for a variety of reasons. The most succinct statement of the criticisms of current regulation under section 404 is that the program is "slow, unpredictable, and unfair" (Executive Office of the President, 1993). In particular, critics point out that the permit program does not allow for administrative appeals of USACE decisions. Property owners and developers complain that the delineation of wetlands has been poorly performed, and is often inaccurate and slow. Decisions to allow or disallow activities often appear arbitrary, and the lack of clear, consistent delineation compounds this perception. Resource preservation advocates, on the other hand, assert that current implementation does little to protect wetlands from development, and share many of the same delineation complaints voiced by the regulated community.

Some observers of wetlands protection view the section 404 program as an unwieldy compromise between development and environmental interests. Wood (1989), for example, contends that the statute was left intentionally vague, due to splits within Congress that made impossible the crafting of a majority to support a strong, pro-environmental statute. Doing so gave the USACE district engineers latitude to protect ecologically fragile wetlands, or allowed engineers to permit the destruction of a wetland when no readily identifiable alternatives were present.

Expansion of the scope and effect of 404 during the late 1970s was muted by USACE and EPA officials. Federal regulators feared a development backlash because section 404 is probably more intrusive than any other form of federal regulation regarding the use and development of private property. In the 1990s, legislation such as the "Property Owner's Bill of Rights," sponsored by Louisiana congressman Billy Tauzin in 1995, took aim at the intrusive nature of wetlands regulation.

The 404 Permit Process

In order for a discharge permit to be granted under section 404, the discharge must meet three criteria. First, the discharge cannot generate any significantly adverse environmental impact. Second, there must be no practicable upland alternative to the wetland site available for the proposed non-water dependent activity. Third, the proposed 404 activity must generally be water dependent. Under USACE regulations, a permit will be granted unless the district engineer determines that granting a permit would be contrary to the public interest. EPA regulations are more stringent, stating that a permit will be denied unless it can be demonstrated such discharge would not have an unacceptable adverse impact.

The permitting process under section 404 appears in figure 3-1. As the figure shows, the process is sequential, allowing for multiple comments and access by interested parties to the decision on any permit. All interested parties—defined as related federal and state agencies, proximate land-owners, community interest groups, and residents—must be notified and provided opportunity to comment. Relevant agencies include not only the USACE and EPA, but also the U.S. Fish and Wildlife Service (USFWS) and the National Marine Fisheries Service (NMFS). The TVA and USCG are also occasionally involved in occasional 404 permitting decisions. These agencies are able to review the development or site proposed for discharge, attend and comment in preapplication meetings between the USACE and the applicant, and comment on permit applications. The USACE then considers the comments of these agencies, along with other vested interests, in rendering a discharge permit decision.

The Corps of Engineers issues a public notice upon receipt of the permit application, and then holds a public comment period, usually lasting between 15 to 30 days. Public hearings may be held on the permit, allowing for a form of procedural due process. The USACE has 90 days from the date of permit application to reach a decision.

Only the Corps of Engineers can issue a permit. The EPA retains the authority to deal with enforcement actions, but has delegated permitting authority to the USACE except in cases of persistent violators. Other agencies are allowed to register comment and objec-

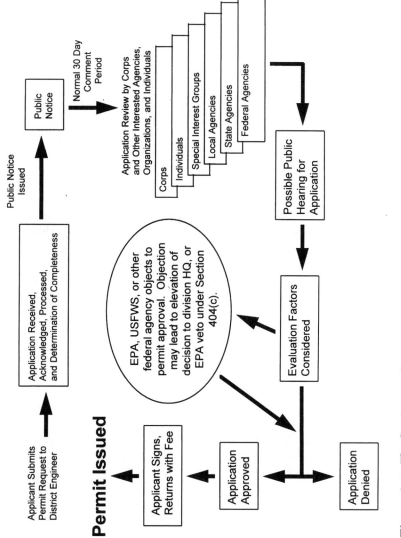

Figure 3-1: The Section 404 Permitting Process

tions to the granting of a permit. The EPA retains final authority to determine if a permit will be issued, and can veto a USACE decision.

Elevation

Although only the Corps of Engineers can issue or deny permits, the other federal agencies are able to affect the issuance of a permit. The EPA can explicitly veto the issuance of an individual permit. When disputes arise between Corps and other agencies, the preferred method of resolving a dispute that extends beyond the review and comment phase is to elevate the dispute to the regional or—eventually—national level. The EPA, USFWS, and the NMFS all retain the ability to elevate a disagreement on the issuance of a permit to the division or national command of the Corps.

If the EPA issues an objection to a permit application, and the USACE issues the permit, the Corps of Engineers must notify the relevant EPA Regional Administrator, who then has 15 days to respond. An agency that objects to the issuing of a permit can then either withdraw the objection, or challenge the permit through elevation. If the permit decision is elevated by the EPA, the EPA Assistant Administrator for Water then seeks review by the Assistant Secretary of the Army for Civil Works to make a final determination.

The EPA Administrative Veto

If the Corps of Engineers decides to proceed with issuing a permit over the objections of the EPA, and the dispute between the USACE and EPA or other resource agencies remain unresolved, the EPA can veto the permit decision. The veto is the final administrative decision of the process. An EPA veto can only be overturned through litigation. Elevation is not a precondition to the exercise of the administrative veto. The EPA, as the responsible agency for implementation of the Clean Water Act, has final responsibility for any permitting decision and derives veto power accordingly. Veto and elevation are rarely used in the section 404 process. The EPA exercised its veto on just seven occasions between 1972 and 1991.

O'Toole (1991) speculates that EPA, the USFWS, and the NMFS wish to maintain cordial relations with USACE. Therefore, they rarely exercise these regulatory prerogatives. Elevation is also costly in terms of time and program reputation. If a permit decision is elevated, administrative time is consumed. Resources that otherwise might be dedicated to effective oversight are consumed. Frequent elevation will extend the review process for applicants. The appearance of a squabbling, fractured regulatory environment would only further erode the confidence of the public in a program already perceived to be time-consuming and beset with problems. For these reasons the relevant agencies have agreed in principle on the issues and conditions that will result in elevation.

The volume of permits compared to resources available for review at the EPA, USFWS, and NMFS also constrain the use of elevation. According to the EPA Inspector General, for region 4 (Atlanta), many permits effectively go unreviewed at the EPA. Elevation is unlikely on many cases because the cases are not examined. At the USFWS, the opposite problem is apparent. Our interviews with state and Federal officials indicated that two things can be expected from the Fish and Wildlife Service on a permit application. The USFWS reviews lots of permits, and the Service's reviewers often issue objections. If the USFWS is in the habit of being overruled in the 404 process, elevating every permit issued over their objections would overwhelm the elevation system. A more likely outcome is that which occurred in Florida, where the relevance of USFWS to the permit process has been diminished, which is a matter we will discuss at greater length in chapter 5.

So, it initially appears that, unlike the dynamic resource that they regulate, the behavior of federal agencies in the wetland protection business has crystalized. Agencies are reverting to expected behavior based on their agency culture, and, as a consequence, while *information* flows within the regulatory structure, it does not lead to substantive policy decisions. Instead, actors play their procedural roles.

Enforcement Provisions and Litigation

The U.S. Army Corps of Engineers (Corps), as the effective street-level federal agency in the implementation of wetland protection, has a variety of substantial policy levers at its disposal. In particular, USACE district engineers may modify, suspend, or revoke any permit in "the general public interest. The modification process occurs based on several options. Modifications through mutual agreement are always the preferred option. If mutual agreement between USACE and the prospective permittee cannot be reached, the USACE district engineer can suspend the permit. A hearing on the decision is held if the permittee requests. Alternatively, if sufficient modifications cannot be made, the permit is revoked.

The Corps is involved in permitting beyond the initial permit decision. The Corps of Engineers can engage in a variety of activities to ensure compliance with section 404 provisions:

- Inspections of work/ activity site.

- Oral or written demands for correction of non-compliance can be made to the permittee.

- Suspension of the permit if non-compliance continues.

- Interagency surveillance and coordination is encouraged.

- Bonds may be required to ensure compliance and "protect the public interest in the waterway," of "sufficient amount to indemnify the government against any loss as a result of corrective action it might take."

- Cease-and-desist orders.

The Corps does not engage in extensive oversight of projects after the permit is issued. Compliance actions are difficult to undertake and the process of periodically reviewing permitted sites detracts from issuing and reviewing new permit applications. This option is not often exercised because of its impact on the speed of the implementing process.

If, in the process of oversight, the Corps detects violations of section 404 standards and/or the particular permit agreement, the USACE district engineer can refer or recommend both criminal and civil litigation. Litigation can be pursued for violation of an existing permit, the failure to obtain a permit, or for proceeding with activity when a permit has explicitly been denied:

- When criminal action is appropriate: (a) punitive action is deemed necessary; (b) future deterrence is essential to maintaining a viable permit program.

- When civil action is appropriate: (a) restoration of the wetland is in the public interest; (b) attempts to secure voluntary compliance have failed; (c) a civil penalty under the Clean Water Act is warranted.

Litigation is referred to the local U.S. Attorney. Citizens can also bring actions for violations under section 404 against individuals or government agencies. Although legal actions for violations of section 404 are rare, substantial fines and even prison terms have been levied for gross permitting violations.

Takings

According to recent figures cited by the White House Office on Environmental Policy, over 75 percent of the wetlands in the lower 48 states are privately held. The Clinton administration has indicated a desire to "avoid unnecessary impacts on [wetlands] landowners" when regulating wetland use and protection (White House, 1993). One of the most common criticisms of wetlands regulation is that it needlessly and unfairly encroaches on private property rights. Opponents of the application of section 404 have argued that the enforcement of the regulation constitutes a regulatory "taking" by the federal government, and therefore entitles the owners to damages and compensation under the fifth amendment (*Lucas v. South Carolina Coastal Commission* [1994]).

Takings occur when the government enforces a regulation that denies certain land uses and thereby decreases the value of the property. Traditional interpretations of takings have held that a taking only occurred when an individual was physically deprived of property by the government. However, legal precedent exists for viewing the activities of the government under section 404 as regulatory takings.

In *Munger v. Kansas* (123 U.S. 623 [1887]), the Supreme Court held that legislation which prevents land use for activities injurious to the public health and public good do not constitute takings. In the words of the Court: "A nuisance is only abated; in the other, unoffending property is taken away from an innocent owner." The Court effectively ruled that the property rights of the owner to develop his land were overridden by the potential negative externality such activity would have on the greater public health. Thirty-five years later, in *Pennsylvania Coal Mine v. Mahon* (260 U.S. 393 [1922]), the Supreme Court opted for a more restrictive definition of taking, stating that "if the regulation goes *too far* [emphasis added] it will be recognized as a taking." When compared to the decision in *Munger*, which effectively closed the door on regulatory takings, the decision in *Mahon* opened up the possibility that a private land owner could pursue compensation for inadvertent economic harm caused by onerous governmental regulation. More recently, in a state case— *Just v. Marinette County* (Wisconsin State Supreme Court, 1966), the Wisconsin courts ruled that a property purchased for the purpose of speculation which was deprived of anticipated value due to regulation did not constitute a taking, because the loss was artificial or speculative rather than real. And, most recently, in *Lucas v. South Carolina Coastal Commission* the Court held that an environmental taking occurs only when *all* economically-beneficial uses of the property are deprived. In fact, since 1994, this has led the Republican majorities in the Congress, along with support from some moderate and conservative Democrats, to adopt legislation restricting takings as well as wetland regulations. The two issues are politically joined, which further reinforces the controversy over wetland regulation.

Federal Implementation of Section 404

Our previous chapters indicate that the implementation of wetland protection regulations by the Corps of Engineers and the EPA has been subject to substantial criticism for more than a decade. Separate reports by the Inspector General of EPA region 4, the EPA headquarters Inspector General, and the General Accounting Office (GAO) identified similar shortcomings with USACE implementation and EPA oversight of the Section 404 program. Our interviews with state regulators uncovered similar criticisms. Although USACE had 404 permitting authority, the EPA remains the responsible party. Therefore, the focus of administrative evaluations ultimately fall on the EPA instead of on USACE with the principal question to be answered: Is the EPA fulfilling its basic legislative and programmatic responsibilities under section 404?

Overview

The Corps of Engineers and EPA share responsibility for developing programmatic guidelines governing 404 implementation; wetlands delineation and identification; permit review; and enforcement. Although functional authority is shared among several agencies, the EPA Office of Water is ultimately responsible for national wetland management and implementation. Wetlands were designated a "high-priority" environmental function in 1984. For the purpose of enforcement of wetlands, the EPA had an annual budget of $10.4 million in 1990, with 105 fulltime staff. In 1991, the budget grew to $18.4 million, and staff resources increased to 155 individuals (78 percent increase in budget, 48 percent increase in staff). Despite the levels of accountability, budget size, and the presence of interagency input and multiple veto points, the GAO estimated that 300,000 acres of wetlands are destroyed every year.

The EPA's Inspector General at the time argues that the section 404 program is "difficult to administer and beset by conflict and controversy." According to the GAO studies, "Program objectives were approached inconsistently or ignored by regional management resulting in a wetlands program that was unpredictable to the regulated public and, therefore, subject to public distrust and criticism" (1990; ii–iii) and "[r]egional wetland programs were permitted to respond to the agenda of regional management rather than commit to the [Bush] Administration's and the Office of Water's program objectives" (1990; iii). The study continued by stating that "[a]s a result of inadequate management control and accountability, wetlands as a whole were not afforded the protection under section 404 as envisioned by the Administrator." To characterize it in the context of the Sabatier's top-down implementation paradigm (see chapter 1), guidelines, procedures, and goals that permeated from the top of the regulatory structure were not being complied with at the bottom. Further, bottom-up discretion was not encouraging the attainment of the general policy goal of no-net-loss.

The GAO and the EPA Inspector General identified two primary areas where USACE implementation and EPA oversight resulted in inferior wetlands protection and inefficient program implementation. First, the EPA and the Corps of Engineers failed to develop and implement comprehensive wetlands protection strategies. Second, a lack of issue resolution exists between the implementing and commenting agencies. In addition, the auditor's report noted eight related issues that undermined the effective implementation of the section 404 program, discussed below.

No Comprehensive Strategy

The Inspector General's reports were highly critical of both the EPA Water Office and the EPA Regional administrators for their failure to oversee effectively the implementation of section 404. According to the audit by the EPA headquarters Inspector General, ineffective control and oversight at the national level allowed regions to set their own wetland priorities. The lack of regional goals, the lack of commitment to wetlands protection and enforcement, and the lack of resources all contributed to problems of wetland eradication. The section 404 program required better oversight, guidance, and interagency coordination to succeed in protecting wetland resources. In evaluating the 404 program, the EPA Inspector General found that EPA and USACE could not develop a comprehensive strategy for a variety of reasons. First, there were no regional data on which to base regulatory decisions, and no regulatory history of the program was ever constructed. Second, the Corps of Engineers demonstrated no consistency in public notice reviews. Third, at the regional level, the EPA failed to exercise statutory authority related to jurisdiction and interagency disputes, especially between EPA, USACE, and the USFWS. The failure of section 404 implementation fit into the classic, top-down model of implementation advanced by Sabatier (1983), Mazmanian and Sabatier (1981), and so many others (see chapter 1): insufficient control and enforcement from the top levels of EPA to the regions contributed to a lack of mission clarity and, ultimately, to the failure of the policy.

At the national level, the lack of national guidelines or an active oversight mechanism from EPA left the Corps of Engineers and the regulated public with the impression that the permit review process was unpredictable and ineffective. This perception led to the assumption of adversarial roles by USACE and EPA. In EPA regions 4, 6, and 7, the failure to target limited resources to the depletion of "most valuable wetlands" resources further exacerbated the problem of resource protection, again reinforcing the failure due to a lack of top-down implementation control.

Lack of Issue Resolution

The lack of issue resolution is the primary result of inter- and intra-agency conflict, especially within the EPA and between the EPA, USACE, and USFWS. There are a variety of unresolved issues, and the principal of these is defining a "wetland." Other basic questions of statutory design, intent, and application remain as well: do the section 404 guidelines developed by the agency serve as thresholds for wetland preservation, or are they simply considerations to be weighed against other factors during the public interest review? Should wetland damage be avoided or simply mitigated? How should one assess the cumulative impact of regulation and degradation on wetlands systems? How should the agencies enforce compliance? What standard and flexibility is assigned local land use? Each of these unresolved issues created general confusion in the 404 program.

Management Direction, Control, and Accountability

The GAO and the EPA Inspector General concluded that many problems with section 404 resulted from ineffective control and a lack of accountability in the program. These management problems were compounded by the delegation of the day-to-day operation of the 404 program to the Corps of Engineers, and the lack of clear communication between regional EPA officials and the USACE districts. Resource limitations at the EPA led to the 1976 Memorandum of Agreement delegating enforcement and permitting to the Corps of Engineers. The decision to delegate this authority to USACE was logical because of USACE's responsibilities under section 10 of the River and Harbors Act, and, in theory, this delegation represented a creative streamlined solution to providing regulation. Unfortunately, the EPA regions have little knowledge of USACE permitting processes, delineation techniques, levels of compliance with the national memorandum of agreement, or the general effectiveness of the 404 program as delegated to the Corps of Engineers. For example, in region 4, the USACE did not inform EPA about repeat violators for enforcement action (General Accounting Office, 1991), though more recent conversations with Corps and EPA reveal an improvement in interagency communication.

In defending the inadequacies of their administration of the 404 program, the EPA Water Policy Office argued ignorance of administrative shortcomings, and ascribed blame for the problems in section 404 to the Corps of Engineers for not notifying the EPA of USACE enforcement actions or violations. This argument did not satisfy the EPA's own Inspector General's office, which countered correctly that the enforcement of section 404 continues to be an EPA responsibility. In the opinion of EPA and GAO evaluators, USACE assumed some enforcement responsibilities as a courtesy to the EPA. The GAO went further by stating that the failure to maintain adequate oversight of Corps activity was "not prudent management" by EPA. The GAO report also concluded that the Environmental Protection Agency can delegate enforcement authority, but not the legal responsibility. In fact, failure of the section 404 program to protect wetlands resources ultimately resides with the EPA, even if that failure was a product of USACE actions. This point in particular is also interesting as it relates to perspectives on implementation. The EPA did not have the necessary resources to directly implement section 404, so the agency delegated the authority to do so to the agency that afforded the most direct access to the target, the Corps of Engineers. From a bottom-up perspective this is indicative of building a system back from the target: find the agencies that bring government most in contact with the regulated entity, and *act through it* (Hjern and Porter, 1982). However, the difference in mission of the USACE and EPA undercut implementation success, which is more indicative of top-down implementation failures (see Goggin *et al.*, 1990, chapter 1).

Unresolved Agency Missions and Goals

Policy differences and varying expectations of the involved agencies undermined the achievement of effective, responsive management of the 404 program. The Corps of Engineers is forced to balance competing value sets in administration and permit decisionmaking. For example, in our conversations with representatives of the states on the Atlantic seaboard, especially in Maryland, it was reiterated that the budgets of USACE district offices are determined in part by the number of permits they process. The incentive structure for local USACE permitters is to process a large quantity of permits as quickly as possible, rather than to pursue more time-consuming quality permit evaluations. The popularity of nationwide and statewide programmatic general permits among Corps of Engineers implementors becomes clear when viewed against this incentive: NPGPs and SPGPs are "one-size-fit-all" permits that capture a variety of approved activities in the waters of the United States. For the issuing agency (USACE) they require relatively little investment of personnel or other resources to process. Conflicts about permit decisions arise mainly in local land-use plans, attempts by the EPA to ensure the preservation of resources, and the USACE attempts to apply best management practices to regulated lands.

The nature of the Corps of Engineers' mission compared to that of the EPA and the other resource agencies also contributes to conflict in the permit process. The Corps of Engineers historically has been in the business of adapting natural resources for human use, creating infrastructure, and developing creative engineering solutions to problems presented by nature. This tradition at the USACE did not include functioning as a resource preservation agency, although its emphasis on that function has increased dramatically since the late 1980s. By way of comparison, the Fish and Wildlife Service is a classic resource-preservation agency. The historic mission of the USFWS has emphasized wetlands preservation longer than any other federal agency, going back to to the Duck Stamp program in the first part of the twentieth century. By its very nature, the world view of the agency is first to protect the resource. Then there is the Environmental Protection Agency. The EPA represents a regulatory approach that emphasizes the minimization of adverse impacts on the environment from development. The lack of common policy goals regarding wetlands either at the various administrative levels within or across agencies leads to inevitable conflict coupled with inconsistent policy outcomes. This conflict is virtually guaranteed to continue because Congress has institutionalized both the development of wetlands and the protection of those resources.

Delineation

As we noted initially in chapter 1, interagency differences are most apparent is in the delineation of wetlands. In practice the Fish and Wildlife Service uses a broader definition of wetland than either the EPA or the Corps of Engineers, although all of the involved agencies were expected to use the same delineation after 1989. As reported by the GAO, "More wetlands could be protected if the Corps delineated wetland boundaries more broadly" (GAO, 1991:32). This is a particularly serious impediment to successful implementation from a top-down perspective. While all of the agencies have an interest in the regulated target—the wetland—their understanding of what constitutes the target differs substantially. This lack of specific, common goal-definition at the bottom is viewed by both top-down and bottom-up frameworks as an impediment to successful implementation. And, it is precisely this problem which often creates problems in both the regulation of wetlands and the process of section 404 assumption.

The Role of 404 Guidelines

An issue related to delineation is the role of section 404 guidelines. The EPA and the USFWS consider the provisions of section 404 *threshold standards* to which the USACE must adhere when making permitting decisions. By contrast, the USACE uses 404 guidelines as *considerations* which are weighed against other factors in the public interest review, and the relative weight of section 404 guidelines vary by proposal (GAO, 1991: 11–12). This particular conflict has started toward resolution. The Fish and Wildlife Service maintains that the "guidelines should be applied as a threshold" rather than as a component of an economic analysis (GAO: 113), while the EPA commented that "the balancing process used by the Corps does not obviate the requirements to comply with the guidelines" (GAO: 105). Starting in 1992, the Corps of Engineers gave added weight to the 404 standards in permit review. But the historic differences of opinion regarding the role played by the section 404 guidelines contributes to the conflict between the USACE and other concerned agencies, and originates in the differing missions and world-views of the Corps of Engineers, the EPA, and the Fish and Wildlife Service. Such a fundamental conflict goes to the core missions of each agency, and and will not be easily resolved as long as these agencies are collectively involved in wetland regulation. And, as long as all are involved in wetland regulation, this threat to implementation success is institutionalized.

Alternatives Analysis

One of the principal conflicts between the EPA and the Corps of Engineers has been the application of alternatives analysis to permit applications. Before a permit is granted for a non-water based activity in a wetland, efforts must be made to identify a suitable "dry" site for that activity, assuming such an alternative site exists. The USACE contends that the examination of alternatives to the sites proposed for permit activity is one part of the balancing and public review process. The EPA and USFWS contend that that the USACE is obliged to avoid any adverse impact on wetlands and encourages the use of alternatives wherever they exist. Resource agencies such as USFWS typically adhere to the following priorities for addressing the potential destruction of wetlands via permitted activities:

- avoidance of wetlands destruction or degradation.

- minimization of impact by permitted activity on wetlands.

- compensation for damage or degradation of wetlands due to permitting activity.

This ordering of goals is central to plans proposed by the states seeking section 404 authority. More recently, the Corps of Engineers sought to adhere to the EPA guidelines regarding alternatives analysis, although evidence of increased recommendation of use of alternatives by USACE is not available, undermining any effort to assess the success of this policy imperative.

Cumulative Impacts

The Department of the Interior (DOI) states that the main problem with the Corps of Engineers approach to impact assessment of wetlands is "the absence of resource goals . . . to restore and maintain the nation's water resources" (GAO, 1990: 30). This shortcoming in particular does not bode well for implementation success, regardless of the intellectual framework used to understand the implementation. A lack of goals, whether articulated from the top or the bottom, increases the likelihood of a fragmented or unfocused implementation.

The lack of data on the impact of previous permitted activities makes the incorporation of a cumulative impacts assessment into future decisions nearly impossible. Because impact data are not currently collected, cumulative effects analysis is not likely for the near future. The USACE has given no indication of accounting for cumulative impacts in the permitting process.

Enforcement

Students of public choice economics have often advanced the argument that one way to avert defection or antisocial behavior is through monitoring (Mueller, 1989). Top-down implementation scholars concur with this argument, consistently finding that aggressive monitoring of both field-level agency actors and of the targets of policy leads to increased implementation success (Mazmanian and Sabatier, 1981; Van Meter and Van Horne, 1975). No aggressive compliance program exists to monitor actions under section 404, and any enforcement that occurs is typically *post hoc* to violations. Conversations with federal water officials and an examination of the previously cited GAO report on section 404 revealed that the EPA regional offices are often not notified by the Corps of Engineers of detected violations of permit applications by repeat violators. The EPA often is unaware of the nature or extent of section 404 violations. As a result, the EPA is not well positioned to deny permits to prior or continuing violators. Occasional inspection by Fish and Wildlife Service field workers will turn up violations, but the USFWS lacks sufficient resources, an explicit agency mandate, or the responsibility to enforce section 404. Moreover, given the marginal role of the Fish and Wildlife Service in the permit review process, the detection of violations by service personnel potentially may be discounted, especially if USFWS personnel become more aggressive. The failure to monitor and communicate violations serves to impede implementing sanctions or using other tools of coercion.

There is reason to limit criticisms of enforcement shortcomings with regard to the implementation of section 404. In order to consider enforcement as a solution, it is first important to establish goals and define criteria for enforcement. Because these two preconditions are lacking in the federal wetlands protection structure, an effort to address enforcement will have a very limited impact on resource protection. This general implementation failure had a variety of states considering other wetland protection options, starting in the late 1980s. The principal option explored by the states was the assumption of federal regulatory authority.

State Assumption of Wetlands Regulation under Section 404

One aspect of the USACE mission in implementing section 404 is to facilitate and promote the assumption of the program by the states. Under regulations established by the Clean Water Act Amendments of 1977, the EPA can allow a state to assume the processing of dredge and fill permits from the Corps of Engineers. In order to qualify for state assumption a state must:

- establish a wetlands discharge-and-fill program which as at least as stringent as the regulations established by EPA and delegated to the Corps of Engineers.

- adhere to a delineation of wetlands at least as rigorous as that used by EPA.

- allow for public comment on permitting decisions.

State assumption of section 404 regulation is technically not a delegation of federal power; rather, the state program replaces federal regulations in waters which are assumable under section 404. The federal program disappears when a state assumes section 404. The applicability of federal statutes such as the Endangered Species Act to permitting decisions also ceases, although state wildlife protection in the permitting program must be at least as stringent as would be applied by U.S. Fish and Wildlife Service regulations. To date, two states—Michigan and New Jersey—successfully have assumed section 404 implementation authority from the USACE. Other states have studied, or are considering, assumption of that authority.

Accountability and State Assumption

A variety of state and national wetland resource organizations advocate state assumption of the section 404 program, both to remedy problems with USACE implementation of the permit program and as part of a move toward broader state wetland management programs. The criticisms of Corps implementation we have observed—delay, uncertainty, possible inconsistency of permit decisions, and the lengthy interagency review process—are among the variety of factors that lead to encouragement of state assumption. And, more generally speaking, a program with broad regulatory scope that is remote to affected populations and beyond their ability to influence can suffer from legitimacy problems in a democratic society and be difficult to enforce (Lowi, 1972). A reformulation of implementation will need to address the consistency and accountability issues that are associated with policy in democratic states. Can state assumption of section 404 authority rectify these problems in wetland regulation?

Assumption: Benefits, Concerns, Limitations

There are several perceived benefits of state assumption of section 404, as well as potential problems. Among the benefits are: enhanced resource management and preservation of wetland resources; timely, consistent, responsive application decisions; and a presumption that agencies will be able to resolve any policy differences. Also, the perception of simplified, timely, consistent decisions under assumption creates the opportunity for stronger commitment to preservation by resource interests.

There are limitations as to what wetlands the states can assume for regulation. The assumability of regulatory authority over a wetland resource is dependent on the water resource to which the wetland is adjacent. Recall, section 404 technically governs water quality. The regulation of the adjacent wetland is implicit in the section. The extension of these regulations to wetlands is derived from the interpretation of the statute and an application of existing water-quality research by the federal courts in the 1970s.

Under current regulations, the USACE regulates three "phases" of waters as defined by the 1976 federal court ruling that expanded Corps jurisdiction beyond the traditional waters regulated under the Rivers and Harbors Act. The assumability of wetlands by a state is dependant on the "phase" of water adjacent to the wetland because the USACE retains jurisdiction over water requiring section 10 permits. Phase I waters are those traditionally navigable waters which USACE has always regulated under the mean-high-water mark test that defines navigable waters of the United States. It includes: (1) all waters currently used for—or susceptible to use for—interstate and foreign commerce; (2) impoundments; (3) the territorial sea; and (4) adjacent wetlands to those waters in (1–3), and those waters defined as navigable under section 10 of the Rivers and Harbors Act of 1899.

In those remaining waters, defined by the USACE as phase II and phase III waters, the Corps of Engineers ceases to process section 404 permits when a state assumes section 404. Instead, the state assumes authority for permit processing, including determining the areas and activities regulated, the processing of individual permits, and enforcement. The federal section 404 program disappears in the phase II and phase III waters and adjacent wetlands, and is replaced by the more rigorous state program. The EPA retains oversight through annual review of the program, and retains the right of review, objection, and the right to make the final determination on the disposition of individual permits for major discharges.

The states obtain expanded wetlands jurisdiction by displacing the Corps of Engineers in some waters under an assumed program. They also obtain a variety of detrimental obligations which accompany 404, and lose the support of a variety of federal resource programs. The state shares jurisdiction of the program with the USACE, but receives no federal funding for the initiation or continued implementation of the program. The states continue to receive federal oversight of the wetlands permitting program from the EPA. The states only obtain jurisdiction over those phase II and phase III waters that lie outside the traditional venue of the Corps of Engineers. The USACE retains all tidal waters and adjacent wetlands, as well as all navigable waters and adjacent wetlands.

The state program must have a scope of jurisdiction at least equivalent to that of the USACE in phase II and phase III waters. The state program must at least regulate the same activities, have adequate enforcement authority to run the permit program and ensure compliance with the guidelines as specified under section 404. After a state has assumed 404, the state program is subject to annual EPA review. The state must submit to the EPA copies of final action on all permits, annual non-compliance reports, and an annual report on the program impact and the integrity of state waters regulated by the state 404 program. The EPA retains review, comment, and veto power over any state decision that is not covered by a national or general permit. Differing expectations of the state program, mission and philosophy might create problems in the public and between state and federal regulation agencies. Other concerns are that assumption does not resolve coordination problems, or that a state which assumes permitting responsibility cannot provide adequate funding. The assumed program does streamline the implementation process in some waters, removing some of the pesky veto points that Pressman and Wildavsky (1973) found so troubling to implementation success. But assumption also creates bifurcated permitting systems within states that agencies and clients may find troubling or confusing.

The Federal Role Under Assumption

The federal role appears to be substantially reduced when a state assumes the section 404 program. The role of the Fish and Wildlife Service and the National Marine Fisheries Service is substantially reduced, and the applicability of their regulations is diminished. The Corps of Engineers is removed from the process, except in phase I waters where the USACE retains jurisdiction under section 10 of the Rivers and Harbors Act. The EPA retains comment, veto, and oversight of the program. Relevant federal agencies must continue to review and comment on discharges involving contaminated materials, discharges in critical environmental areas, and major discharges. They may comment on other permitting decisions, but are not required to by statute or regulation.

Conclusions About State Assumption: Questions Remain

Proponents of wetland preservation have expressed concerns over the potential expansion of delegation of the 404 program. In particular, these concerns surround the minimum regulatory standards the EPA will sanction for assumption. If the EPA relaxes standards in order to encourage state assumption of the 404 program, what will be the consequences for the shape of state regulation? Will developers encourage states to assume 404 in order to escape more onerous federal regulation? Does state assumption work as a policy choice for a state? Why is the process of assumption unattractive to many states? What factors are related to decisions by states to consider or pursue assumption?

Other questions remain as well: Does state assumption facilitate better implementation of wetland regulation and protection? Are the concerns of state agencies, environmental activists, and the regulated public regarding section 404 addressed in assumption? And, finally, are there structural, legal, political, or other problems associated with section 404 that affect the *process* of implementing state assumption?

4

Two Tales of Assumption:
Michigan and New Jersey

What can the federal government do to help states interested in assumption? The most obvious answer is that all federal agencies must accept assumption as a viable option.

New Jersey regulator

S tate assumption of the 404 wetlands program from the federal government is being promoted by some as a solution to many of the problems with current wetlands protection. The experience of state assumption of the section 404 program in Michigan and New Jersey, the only two states to take over the federal section 404 program, reveals valuable lessons about the incentives, actions, and consequences confronting states as they consider federal programs. States considering assumption of the 404 program should understand that the assumption process is neither easy nor fast, and may not convey immediate benefits to the assuming state. The assumption process needs to be entered into soberly and cautiously, and requires a great deal of work on the part of the parties involved.

This chapter is divided into three sections. First, we discuss the experience of Michigan in assuming and then operating a state 404 program. As the only assumption experience for a decade, the Michigan program has typically been viewed as a model for other states considering assumption (O'Toole, 1991; Bostwick, 1989). The lack of extensive political influences in the process of Michigan's assumption also contributes to its image as a model. The next part of the chapter deals with the controversial but ultimately successful New Jersey assumption of the 404 program. As non-controversial as Michigan's assumption was, the New Jersey experience was described by an outside observer as "a textbook example of how not to do assumption." Nonetheless, valuable lessons emerged from New Jersey's experience that were not lost on regulators in states that were still considering assumption. Finally, we examine the lessons learned from the Michigan and New Jersey programs as they relate to questions of implementation.

Michigan

The state of Michigan extensively regulated wetlands prior to assumption of the section 404 program in 1984. Michigan first started regulating the dredge, fill, and discharges into the Great Lakes in 1966. In 1976, the state developed a joint permitting program with the Corps of Engineers, Detroit District. Michigan has had an assumed discharge and fill permitting operation in force since March 1984. They operated a trial wetlands permitting operation under a grant from the USFWS. Enacting legislation was initially proposed in 1979, and full enactment was passed in 1983.

The permitting program in Michigan operates under a negotiated agreement with the EPA and the USACE. These agreements are fairly loose, and the EPA agreement was due to be renegotiated in 1995. There are approximately 5 million acres of wetlands in Michigan, comprising approximately 30 percent of the state. These wetlands are more heavily concentrated in the Upper Peninsula. Wetlands are extremely scattered in Michigan, and a veteran Michigan permitting official summed ou their problem thus: "It is impossible to build a 200-acre golf course in Michigan and not hit a wetland. There are little pockets of water everywhere; it's just an attribute of glacial geography." Michigan has a large number of phase II and phase III waters (see chapter 2), and therefore the incentive structure to take over section 404 was substantial: the state would receive primary regulatory authority over most wetlands in the state that were previously covered by section 404.

"A Success Story"

Michigan implementors think that the Michigan program is highly successful. There was no litigation over the Michigan assumption—attributed by all involved parties to the low profile of wetland issues in the early 1980s—and the state only has two publicized implementation failures out of over 30,000 permit cases. One of these cases has been resolved, and the other is in court. The experience of the first public dispute marked the only instance of gubernatorial intervention in the permitting process. The political outcome of that dispute worked to the advantage of the state agency, and effectively deterred future gubernatorial intervention.

> O'Toole (1991: 191) succinctly summarizes the path to Michigan assumption thus: [w]ith the 1977 changes in federal legislation regarding 404 . . . it became obvious that the Corps' 404 permitting efforts would spread further inland and involve a significantly increased workload for permit applications. Citizens would thus have to obtain two different permits and become involved in a substantially heavier regulatory burden. Very quickly thereafter the state began to consider the possibility of seeking 404 assumption and unifying the permit process. The state had been proud of its performance in permitting for wetlands and believed that it should improve on the federal government's regulatory performance with 404 by seeking assumption authority. As early as 1978 the state began to consider assumption and to work on a variety of tasks leading up to the EPA decision in 1984 to allow the state-assumed program to begin implementation.

The Michigan program is an example of a deliberate, measured approach to state assumption. The state was deeply involved in wetland regulation, and anticipated the negative consequences of duplicate regulatory regimes in the state. Rather than rushing into assumption, the state worked with the EPA and other federal agencies to develop a program that could ensure the levels of protection sought by the EPA and maximize state authority.

O'Toole also observed that Michigan had a variety of other advantages entering the assumption process. The state had a history of wetland regulation. The legislature was particularly pro-environment in the 1970s, and Governor James J. Blanchard was a strong proponent of state assumption, reinforcing the prospects for successful assumption (Sabatier, 1983). The state wetlands program was already well-funded. Perhaps, of greatest importance, the Michigan Department of Natural Resources (MDNR) had a reliable inventory of wetland resources in the state, which reduced start-up costs and expedited the delineation of state wetland resources. All of the elements identified by Sabatier and Mazmanian as necessary for a successful implementation were in place: resources, leadership, and capacity.

The state currently maintains a joint application process with the Corps of Engineers. When the state receives a permit application, it determines the jurisdiction of the waters, and then forwards appropriate applications to the USACE. According to Harrington and Kennedy (1988), this program reduces paperwork and costs in the application process, and eliminates a great deal of duplication.

Michigan Assumption

Michigan began the process of assumption almost immediately after the passage of Michigan's Wetlands Protection Act in 1979. This legislation contained language that authorized the state to pursue assumption of the section 404 program. Starting in October 1980 and lasting through late 1982, the state and the USFWS, developed section 404 assumption documents to be sent to EPA. The Michigan Department of Natural Resources (MDNR), EPA, and USACE conducted a demonstration feasibility program to prove state competence in administering section 404. On October 26, 1983, Governor Blanchard requested state assumption of the 404 dredge-and-fill program. Technical differences between the federal and state programs were worked out during the next year, and permit program assumption for Michigan occurred in August 1984.

Memorandum of Agreement

A state-assumed section 404 program is governed by a negotiated set of expectations and obligations called a memorandum of agreement (MOA). The MOA spells out the policy goals and obligations of the state and the federal agencies. The compliance with the MOA is a condition for continuation of the state-assumed program. The memorandum of agreement between Michigan and the EPA has five key points, which illustrate the expectations of the EPA from any assuming state:

- The State must take timely action against section 404 violators;

- EPA/USFWS/USACE shall review and comment on issuance or denial to MDNR on contaminated material discharges, critical environmental or historical areas, and "major discharges";

- State submits every final action to EPA;

- The state must submit quarterly non-compliance reports to EPA (not rigorously enforced);

- Michigan must submit an annual assessment report.

The principal functions of the Michigan MOA are to establish a process of monitoring, feedback, and oversight of the program, and to clearly specify the review and oversight mechanisms that allow federal agencies to continue their comment on state permitting decisions.

Advantages and Disadvantages

In reviewing both the written record of the Michigan permitting program and considering the responses in our interviews with Michigan officials, a high degree of administrative success is evident. Among the benefits of the Michigan program noted by both advocates and critics are: the reduction of time delays in the permit process; staff site inspection of every complete application for a permit, including sites and activities previously covered by nationwide permits; management and protection of state natural resources; lessened USACE influence on state inland waterways; incorporation of section 404 into a consolidated permit process that considers impacts besides those regulated under 404; requirement of one permit application and the issuance of joint public notices where the state and the USACE have joint jurisdiction; reduction of duplication of effort between federal and state agencies; and the presence of an administrative appeals process, which is absent from the

USACE 404 permit process (Harrington and Kennedy, 1988). It is quite a laundry list, as are the disadvantages of state assumption of the section 404 program: loss of dual federal/state enforcement capability; a requirement that the state must formally exhaust its enforcement capability before referring violations to the EPA; the belief that the EPA holds state implementors and state programs to a higher standard than that which the USACE is held; additional time and resources needed to design a state assumption plan in accordance with *all* EPA regulations; and, the political vulnerability, both in the legislative appropriations process and in the enforcement of state statutes (see also Wisconsin Department of Environmental Resources, 1993). We discuss these consequences in greater detail below.

Reduction of Time Delays

O'Toole (1991) has argued that one rationale for examining implementation is to increase the efficiency with which the government transacts its business, both in terms of the time in which it takes to complete tasks, and in terms of reducing the costs associated with achieving successful implementation. In these respects the assumed Michigan program constitutes a definite improvement in the process implementation of discharge-and-fill permitting.

Under Michigan Law, the deadline for a permit decision is 90 days from the date the application is completed; if a public hearing is necessitated, the permit decision clock starts with the date of the hearing. For the first six years of the Michigan program, the Corps of Engineers had no time limit on permit decisions; now they must adhere to a 90-day time clock. Under the current regime, if the Michigan Department of Natural Resources fails to reach a decision within 90 days, the permit is granted automatically. The adoption of a 90-day clock has reduced the confusion in the regulated community concerning the time-factor in permitting. According to state regulators, the expedient nature of state activity created confusion when an applicant requires federal and state permits (applications for activities in Phase I waters). Permit applicants, on obtaining their state permit approval, often were frustrated by the inability of federal regulators to expedite those decisions. In addition, the state's 90-day for the MDNR clock expires before the USACE clock, due to technicalities concerning when the respective clocks' start. The state could reach a decision before the USACE review is complete, or grant a permit by default when USACE still has time to reject or approve the application (Bostwick, 1989). It was therefore possible for two agencies with similar missions to look at exactly the same policy decision and reach conflicting decisions, mainly because of a lack of coordination.

Although the state program has substantially more staff resources than the previous USACE program, the obligations of expanded jurisdiction and inspection, as well as the requirements of the memorandum of agreement consume staff resources. Bostwick (1989) noted that reporting and documenting compliance for the EPA quarterly reports consumes a substantial amount of staff time. Indeed, over half of the time of the Michigan Division of Water's 53 staffers is dedicated to section 404 permit review. Most of the funding for both Michigan's assumed program and other water projects come from the general appropriation, leaving the program potentially vulnerable to legislative initiatives in the appropriations process; over time this constitutes a threat to the MDNR's assumed program.

Scope of Inspection and Activities Regulated

The Michigan program covering section 404 issues a consolidated permit that encompasses activities regulated by nine state and four federal statutes. Michigan field staff inspect all permit application sites, including applications for minor activities which were previously issued under the nationwide permits. One benefit of this requirement is that the impact of previously unlimited activities in low-flow headwaters and adjacent wetlands are reduced, in part because the state is able to bring substantially more resources to bear than the Corps of Engineers. In 1989, the USACE had only five field staff for the entire state, compared to 28 field staff for the Michigan Department of Natural Resources. By 1994, the MDNR staff had expanded to over 40 field staffers. Clearly assumption brought more resources to support implementation, which, according to all of the major theoretical perspectives on implementation discussed in chapter 1, will increase the likelihood of implementation success.

The most significant extension of state regulation beyond the scope of the section 404 regulations concerns wetlands drainage. Under section 404, the Corps of Engineers could regulate discharges and filling activities in waters and adjacent wetlands, but could not regulate the drainage of wetlands. The Michigan program requires a state permit to drain wetlands, thereby extending wetlands protection. Further, provisions exist in the state law for drainage of isolated wetlands and wetlands used for "minor" agricultural activity; such waters and wetlands are not covered under federal law (Brown, 1989).

The elimination of nationwide permits in state-assumable waters substantially increased the scope of state inspection and enforcement, as well as the application of state environmental review criteria. Before state assumption, 70 percent of permits issued by the USACE were classified as nationwides, and an additional 22 percent of permits were issued as general permits. Reviewing minor projects allows Michigan implementors to control for cumulative effects of these minor activities and "enhance comprehensive management and protection of state resources" (Bostwick, 1989).

Reduction of Duplication and Administrative Appeals

State assumption of the section 404 discharge-and-fill program reduced the regulatory burden on most of the affected public, and created avenues for appeal that were absent from the existing USACE permitting process. The advantages of one-stop permitting are clear from the perspective of transaction costs and convenience. Moreover, the existence of a streamlined process that allows for administrative appeals—rather than judicial hearings—builds confidence in the program among the regulated public. When the USACE denies a permit, the only recourse for the applicant is the courts. The inclusion of the administrative appeal internalize permitting disputes and saves the applicant and the state unnecessary legal costs. Michigan and federal regulators both acknowledge that this program has facilitated communication and cooperation between enforcement officials and policy targets, and made the section 404 permitting experience less adversarial.

Loss of Dual State/Federal Enforcement

Michigan implementors themselves admit that "the most significant drawback to the section 404 assumption is the loss of dual state and federal enforcement capabilities" (Bostwick, 1989). The state currently takes the lead on most enforcement actions, although the EPA has requested that some major violations be forwarded to the regional office covering Michigan (region 5). Part of the problem with assumption enforcement is that prosecution or appeals through the federal courts occurs only after state judicial actions are exhausted.

A related complication is that enforcement of the state law occurs in the local jurisdiction (county), where the extent of prosecution is subject to the political will of the local states' attorney (Brown, 1989). The stringency of judicial enforcement of violations of section 404 in Michigan is, therefore, variable.

Higher Standards for Assumption

There are no indications of regret among Michigan officials regarding assumption of 404 authority, and likewise no expressed desire to give the permitting program back to the USACE. Michigan water quality officials note a variety of factors which complicated the assumption process, and indicate that these would make the process of assumption less attractive in the 1990s than in it was in 1979. The two particular factors which Michigan implementors note is also a recurring theme in the other states examined in this study: first, the EPA holds the state to a higher standard of behavior and regulatory attainment than it does its own program run through the USACE; second, designing a wetlands protection assumption program in accordance with all EPA regulations is extremely time consuming. In applying for section 404 assumption, the Michigan officials viewed many EPA-requested changes to be "nitpicking." Furthermore, the standard that the EPA held the proposed Michigan plan to was far more rigorous than the actual Corps of Engineers implementation experience in Michigan or in the rest of the nation.

Michigan in Summary

The Michigan assumption can be characterized as an implementation success on several levels. The state-assumed program successfully supplanted the national program. The state program delivers enforcement to more selected targets, and does so in an expedient fashion. The federal government retains a mechanism to actively oversee the actions of the state program, thereby ensuring compliance with top-level goals, while also allowing sufficient discretion to state implementors. Indeed, the attitude of state-level implementors is that they effectively have an autonomous program.

And, the experiences of Michigan in changing from the national 404 program, to a state-assumed 404 program, reinforce many of the "second-generation" research assumptions made regarding successful policy implementation. Political leaders, field level implementors, and involved agencies all shared a common goal, even if their reasons for seeking the same outcome differed. Priorities were clearly defined, resources were available to facilitate implementation of the new program, and all of the involved actors were highly motivated to see a successful process implementation of assumption.

Michigan can also be viewed as a bottom-up success. In this first attempt at state assumption, the policy goals of state implementors were met by assumption. The regulated community was to have a more efficient, streamlined program for regulating wetlands use. Permit review was expedited and, unlike in the next case we examine, the reasons for pursuing assumption had little to do with either the ability of the national government to implement policy, or with some desire among interest groups to limit the scope of regulation. Instead, the goal was smoothing implementation at the street-level for the targets of regulation.

New Jersey

The other state to successfully complete assumption is New Jersey. The Michigan experience is characterized by harmony and the aura of success. By comparison, New Jersey's assumption experience was contentious, and in particular reveals problems in the implementation of assumption that are a product of communication and competing agency priorities. The basis of New Jersey's wetland policy is the state's Freshwater Protection Act (NJFPA) of 1987. The law was passed with the expressed intention of assuming the federal 404 program; the state did not have a freshwater wetlands law before 1987. The wetland legislation introduced was designed as a companion to the state Coastal Waters Protection Program. The language of the NJFPA mandated state assumption of the 404 program within one year of its enactment.

Unfortunately for state program designers, the implementation of state assumption took considerably longer than one year. Final assumption occurred in March 1994, almost seven years after the state initially enacted the NJFPA.

Public and political resistance to the law was substantial at the time legislation authorizing assumption was passed. Only drastic action by Governor Thomas Kean, a national leader in wetland protection, made the initiation of assumption possible. As O'Toole (1991: 196) noted "the circumstances [of New Jersey assumption] also suggest that a highly active state response requires unusual levels of political and financial resources, and may provoke not-insignificant levels of resistance," a finding consistent with implementing controversial programs that have regulatory or redistributive functions (see also Lowi, 1972). This is definitely the case in the experience of New Jersey, and as our discussion of the cases examined in chapters 5 will show, other states that have considered assumption have been deterred by the threat of a divisive political debate; this particular circumstance is often viewed as a traditional barrier to implementation success.

The principal objection to the assumption of section 404 by New Jersey from outside the state political community was from the USFWS. The Fish and Wildlife Service contended that New Jersey was [and continues to be] unable to perform the function of permitting for section 404 as effectively as, or preserve resources as well as, the Corps of Engineers and EPA. New Jersey officials contended that prior communications from USFWS to the state indicated that USFWS staff felt New Jersey's efforts went beyond those of the Corps of Engineers and that the Service's did not adequately protect wetland resources. One perspective on USFWS resistance, held by state water policy officials, is that local USFWS staff perceived the decentralization of permitting away from the Federal agencies as part of a turf battle. As federal agencies continue to confront increased demands for cuts in spending, the possibility of losing budget is enhanced as agency activities are assumed by the states. Likewise, USFWS officials may view state assumption as a threat to their position in the policy hierarchy, or as a threat to their ability to fulfill the agency mission of the Service, especially the Endangered Species Act.

The state of New Jersey anticipated substantial litigation when section 404 assumption was approved. Conversations with New Jersey implementors revealed the belief that the Fish and Wildlife Service was threatened by the reduction of its jurisdiction in New Jersey. To halt implementation of the proposed assumption, the USFWS was expected to persuade its allies in environmental groups such as the Environmental Defense Fund (EDF) to bring suit against the state. These allegations are only hearsay, and were not substantiated in conversations with either the EDF or USFWS. The lack of any challenge to the New Jersey law indicates that the possibility of challenge has been preempted. Whether this is a result of the changes in Washington—including the Republican control of Congress since 1995—is uncertain. Even without a partisan change in Washington, the USFWS may not have been positioned to bring suit. The Clinton administration and the EPA still support state assumption of 404. Rumors that the Fish and Wildlife Service would persuade the EDF to pursue litigation against New Jersey appear to be unfounded.

"Assumption? Don't do it unless you have to."

New Jersey permitting officials described at length the political dynamic surrounding attempts by the USFWS to block state assumption. When the Fish and Wildlife Service failed to block 404 assumption in New Jersey, state implementors contended that the USFWS used its "friends" in the EDF to hinder implementation. The blocking strategy was based on the Fish and Wildlife Service's contention that the New Jersey law did not guarantee protection of wildlife under the Federal Endangered Species Act. Subsequent to this protest by the USFWS, many environmental groups that initially supported assumption began to oppose it, although as we noted above, no other environmental challenges were forthcoming.

The Freshwater Protection Act was pushed through by retiring Republican Governor Kean during 1988 and 1989. Kean was long associated with the wetland issue, including service as the chairman of the National Wetlands Policy Forum. He subsequently emerged as an advocate of state wetland planning as the best means of preserving the resource. Kean opted to make wetlands his legacy to New Jersey before retiring after a second term. Kean had sought to implement a strong environmental regulation package early in his first term (1983). As with most legislative initiatives, multiple forms of legislation were offered, including an alternative bill that was perceived as more "builder-friendly." The primary protest to the implementation of a New Jersey State wetland program was that such a program would further increase the bureaucracy in the 404 permit process, thereby impeding the processing of applications for discharge-and-fill permits.

The deadlock continued until 1987. On June 8, Governor Kean issued an executive mandate refusing to allow any wetlands permits to be issued by the state until a comprehensive state bill was passed by the legislature. Because no one in the state was sure what actually constituted a wetland, new construction came to a virtual halt. By the end of the month, the legislature passed a comprehensive wetlands protection package that expanded state wetlands regulations beyond the federal scope and called for state assumption of the 404 discharge and fill program.

The NJFPA exceeds federal wetlands standards in several areas, and the act has been cited by numerous wetlands experts as a comprehensive wetlands protection statute (see Meeks and Runyon, 1990). The statement of purpose of the act declares that

[I]t is in the public interest to establish a program for the systematic review of activities in and around freshwater areas designed to provide predictability in the protection of freshwater wetlands; that it shall be the policy of the state to preserve the purity and integrity of freshwater wetlands from random, unnecessary or undesirable alteration or disturbance; and that to achieve these goals it is important that the state expeditiously assume the freshwater wetlands permit jurisdiction currently exercised by the United States Army Corps of Engineers" (Freshwater Protection Act of 1987).

The assumption of 404 was a logical step because, under every possible environmental condition, anyone requiring a federal permit would also require a state permit, and some individuals who might be exempt from federal permits would still require state permits. State assumption under the new law would lead to stream-lined, one-stop shopping for permits to fill or construct around New Jersey-defined wetlands. The state targeted assumption for one year after the statute became law, in July 1988. This policy decision would prove to be problematic for the state as the assumption application review proceeded.

The scope of the New Jersey law is broader than the provisions of section 404. The state office that regulates 404-type activities such as dredge and fill also covers all other environmental impacts, such as pilings and vegetation. The state office consolidates not only vertical wetlands regulation functions from the USACE, but also takes over various functions of USFWS. To obtain a permit, a project must meet nine criteria established in the law, including water-dependency; the lack of practicable alternatives; and not degrading the wildlife, water quality, or effluent standards of the state.

In order to maintain the level of protection afforded to wetlands resources by related Federal statutes such as the Endangered Species Act, the New Jersey legislature incorporated language into the legislation setting the standards of protection for the New Jersey wetlands protection program. The state explicitly maintained the oversight relationship of federal agencies such as the Fish and Wildlife Service in order to minimize the loss of resource protection. In addition, the state's own endangered species law has a longer list and covers more species than does the counterpart federal law.

The current governor of New Jersey, Christine Todd Whitman, indicated upon assuming office her desire to rescind the state provisions that exceed federal minimum standards. Although at the time of our interviews in 1994 state regulators indicated that business interests were lining up to "hit the law" (the words of one state regulator), no such change has been forthcoming. Whitman made an issue of the permit program during her first campaign, against incumbent Democrat Jim Florio, asking "Why does New Jersey need a law stronger than that of the federal government?" An internal memo from the governor's office red-lined provisions to be deleted or amended from the existing law. However, no legislation has been passed to weaken the state-assumed program, and interviews with state legislators on the environmental committees of the New Jersey Assembly and Senate revealed no plans to amend the state law as of late 1995. And, in her reelection campaign, Whitman was unable to emphasize wetlands, being under pressure to justify her own record in office during a tough reelection fight.

Different Standards

In chapter 3 we discussed the policy standards problem related to section 404. The EPA, USACE, and USFWS had different and conflicting criteria for what constituted "acceptable" activities under the 404 permit. This problem emerged again in the negotiation over the New Jersey Memorandum of Agreement to assume section 404. In fighting for final assumption, the principle barrier New Jersey faced was attempting to defend their actual field implementation against the ideal federal standard. The USFWS was rigid in demanding New Jersey comply with the federal *ideal*, even as federal implementors in New Jersey fell short of the quality of *actual* implementation by the state.

An example of this problem is a field test where state implementors, in approving a driveway permit, discovered a rare plant growth (swamp pink) downstream of the driveway which was unaffected by the permit and undetected by federal regulators. They notified the Fish and Wildlife Service, who tracked the swamp pink back to the permit zone, and then proceeded to lambast the state and EPA for threatening endangered plant life. The USFWS objected to the permit and program based on this decision. According to New Jersey regulators, the Corps of Engineers was prepared to issue the permit and either was not aware of, or failed to notify the USFWS about, the presence of the swamp pink. Subsequent negotiations with the FWS about the state assumption of 404 often returned to this case as an indication of the inadequacies of the state propgram.

The conflict between the USFWS, EPA, and New Jersey turned into a public-relations fiasco for the EPA and the state, and was a public-relations coup for the USFWS. Besides "local staff problems," the Fish and Wildlife Service was able to force a better deal for itself in the Memorandum of Agreement than would have otherwise been the case, thanks to the interest group influence brought to bear ostensibly on the agency's behalf. The final observation of another state official was telling: "EPA just caved in to everything Fish and Wildlife wanted." Clearly the political cover and spirit of cooperation that was evident a decade earlier in Michigan was absent from the New Jersey assumption experience.

This case underscores one of the major problems associated with the operation of the section 404 program: species protection and the problem of verification. If a detailed survey for potentially endangered species is made, permitting is delayed. If the survey is rushed, potentially erroneous conclusions may be reached due to the difficulty of identifying rare or endangered species. Such an oversight can lead to future litigation. An example cited by state officials was the bog turtle. Bog turtles are not protected under federal law, but are on the list for consideration. As such, they are protected by New Jersey's endangered species law. Identifying bog turtle nesting grounds and habitat is difficult because the turtle is a burrowing creature, and is readily visible in April and May. For ten months of the year identification of active habitat is more difficult. If the state were to be held to the most rigorous standard for delineation of wetlands, then permit decisions for areas that *might* host turtle nesting grounds could only be made based on data gathered in April and May, which would lead to significant delays in the processing of permit applications, as well as substantial complaint and possible political action by the regulated public.

The New Jersey Application: How Things Are Not Done

A state permit official, who has worked closely with assumption since its inception, admitted that New Jersey was "not ready for assumption. Maybe we were naive, or didn't know what we were in for." The official noted multiple "distractions" to assumption. Essentially, the state ran into three problems within their application as sent to the EPA. First, in June 1988, as the state submitted the initial application to the EPA for 404 assumption, a new set of regulations were issued which were substantially different from the rules under which New Jersey made application. The initial application was returned as incomplete, and New Jersey officials were informed the application required substantial alteration; the EPA offered direction for changes to the application. Second, in 1990, New Jersey went back to the EPA with a revised application, and asked, in effect, "where are the gaps in our application"? In response to the state's request, the EPA directed New Jersey to address three problems in their assumption document:

- The definition of waters of the United States was different from that used by the EPA. In creating the application, part but not all of the definition of waters of the United States was included. By excluding certain waters, New Jersey would have left a loophole allowing some federally-defined wetlands to slip through the state law. Because state 404 assumption requires a law and definition at least as strict as that of the federal government, this provision was obviously unacceptable.

- The New Jersey plan included no provision for public notice of the intent to issue a permit, or of public comment. This provision was necessary under the federal statute, and probably would ultimately have been required by the New Jersey Sunshine Law.

- The New Jersey plan contained no confidentiality proviso. Certain industry or trade information might require confidentiality in order to maintain fair competition conditions guaranteed under federal trade regulations.

New Jersey then submitted a new, revised assumption application, the draft of which was sent in October 1992 to the federal agencies concerned with New Jersey's assumption. The story of how each agency and its affiliate offices reacted to the New Jersey application is a case example of varying and different reactions based on mitigating external influences, and reinforces the importance of the political climate and the goals of various actors to achieving successful implementation. The response of those agencies also provides further evidence of the problems presented by ineffective communication among actors when seeking efficient, effective implementation.

Corps of Engineers

The USACE was not involved in the early stages of the New Jersey assumption process. Two Corps of Engineers districts, New York and Philadelphia, divide jurisdiction over New Jersey, and both districts report to the North Atlantic Division headquarters in New York City. New Jersey primarily encountered resistance to assumption of section 404 permitting from the New York district office. Although the division office was negotiating a memorandum of agreement with New Jersey, at the same time, the subordinate district office in New York was attacking the New Jersey plan. Ironically enough, New Jersey officials expected little trouble from either the two USACE district offices or the division headquarters. This erroneous assumption was based on the historic lack of Corps of Engineers activity in the northern part of the state, which is covered by the New York district.

The Corps of Engineers was not heavily involved in hands-on enforcement of permitting under section 404. New Jersey state officials suggested that USACE enforcement in northern New Jersey was lax at best, and often sloppy. They maintained that the Corps of Engineers often issued permits to sites under national general permits that should not have even qualified. When state enforcement officials noted such departures from regulatory consistency by the Corps of Engineers in New York district, they were often rebuked or ignored by that district office.

Because the New York district faced budget and personnel cuts, it is conceivable that district-level staff viewed the New Jersey assumption as a threat to their turf. This may be especially so if, as New Jersey officials contend, the Corps of Engineers was not properly executing their mission. An appropriate analogy drawn by an anonymous state official was that "Corps was sitting on Manhattan throwing [nationwide] permits out the window toward New Jersey," reflecting in extreme fashion the differences in agency attitude toward the role of the program.

U.S. Fish and Wildlife Service and Environmental Interests

The main opposition confronting New Jersey in assuming and consolidating permitting authority under section 404 came from the Fish and Wildlife Service. A senior state regulator asserted that assumption would have gone "much faster if not for the Fish and

Wildlife roadblock." Not unlike the disagreement between New Jersey and the New York district office of USACE, the problem appeared to be a power struggle between the USFWS and the state over the Fish and Wildlife Service's capacity to stop wetland development projects. A permitting official at the New Jersey Department of Natural Resources observed that "[USFWS] can stop anything. They stopped dams, bridges, you name it. They are very powerful." Another EPA official had previously characterized FWS as the "800-pound gorilla" of environmental protection.

Yet, New Jersey officials did not anticipate a problem with the Fish and Wildlife Service's review of the state's assumption plan. The USFWS had been inactive in New Jersey, and the provisions of the New Jersey law actually are tougher (on paper) on endangered and proposed endangered species protection than the federal laws. More species were covered, and—as was the case in Michigan—the state potentially could put more people into the field to enforce its provisions. In addition, the state required a habitat buffer of 150 feet (transition area) between an endangered species and any proposed development. A New Jersey Division of Water official summed up the attitude of state regulators thus: "we thought they wouldn't have a problem; we do more" than is required under federal law to protect threatened and endangered species. This was not the case.

New Jersey voluntarily pre-cleared its application in October 1992. Soon, NJDNR officials got "rumblings" that the Fish and Wildlife Service was unhappy with the application. Ernie Hahn, an assistant administrator in the New Jersey program, contacted the New Jersey office of the U.S. Fish and Wildlife Service to set up a meeting with those regulators in order to iron out the problems and move forward with assumption. Hahn argued that the USFWS senior official responsible for New Jersey allegedly was upset and confused that a "low-level" implementor such as Hahn would attempt to call him for a meeting; officials at the FWS do not recall this dispute in the same way. Regardless, as a result, the administrator of the New Jersey program intervened to contact USFWS and scheduled a conference that eventually took place in May 1993, and helped lead to the final resolution of state-federal conflict over the assumption MOA.

Although the Fish and Wildlife Service continues to have an active review role in the consolidated program, the perception at New Jersey's Department of Environmental Protection (NJDEP) is that the USFWS perceived that its broad powers were jeopardized by the state assumption of wetland permitting authority. While conversations with USFWS staff indicate that they do perceive their role in

New Jersey to be diminished, New Jersey state officials contend that the opposite is the case. Before consolidation, the USFWS reviewed about 50 New Jersey permits annually. Approximately 500 permit applications per year are theoretically subject to Fish and Wildlife Service review. The USFWS, according to New Jersey officials, is obtaining a more thorough review of New Jersey wetlands habitats now than was the case under the old program.

State officials maintained that the May 1993 meeting produced a very adverse reaction on the part of the Fish and Wildlife Service. In essence, they suggested that the USFWS asked "Why do you want assumption?" After state officials offered their explanation that existing state law required assumption—rendering the previous question moot—their Fish and Wildlife Service counterparts persisted in attempting to persuade state officials to instead pursue a statewide general permit under section 404 provisions. In response, the New Jersey officials countered that the SPGP was unacceptable for two reasons: First, the legislative mandate did not call for application for a statewide permit, and instead mandated assumption of the permitting program. Second, a statewide permit would not reduce the layers of government involved in the permitting process (an attractive feature of assumption). Instead, in the minds of New Jersey implementors, the SPGP merely replicated federal efforts on the state level, thereby adding more government.

Laying aside for a moment the contentious, politicized climate surrounding the assumption to this point, it is fair to say that the USFWS had a valid objection and a reasonable question. New Jersey's rationale for assumption was essentially legislative fiat, with culpability also ascribed to the former governor: the state legislature was compelled to pass legislation by the governor, and legislation was enacted that created a legislative mandate to assume the federal program. Our subsequent analyses of Florida, Maryland, and a variety of other states indicates that the option advanced by the USFWS was a viable one which reduced duplication in the permit process and also reduced Corps involvement in direct implementation. It is a reasonable stepping stone toward full assumption, and reflects the potential wisdom of incrementalchange in policy.

The USFWS subsequently responded to the preclearance assumption application by issuing a critique and response to the "problems" in the application. The USFWS also issued a response to a variety of local and state environmental groups (see also Lockwood, 1994). The USFWS critique argued that New Jersey assumption would actually harm environmental quality and result in less protection of fragile wildlife and rare species. Not surprisingly, the

NJDNR disputed this conclusion. Independent confirmation of the New Jersey viewpoint comes from the negotiations between the state and environmental groups. As New Jersey negotiated with Fish and Wildlife Service and environmental groups, one of the principal local environmental officials stood up and said to the individuals siding with the USFWS "I don't care what you say, the state is doing a better job" with species and wetlands protection than the federal agencies. Other activists disagreed, indicating a lack of unity in the environmental interest group community.

New Jersey officials asserted that the USFWS opposed the New Jersey plan because it would reduce Fish and wildlife Service's administrative responsibility in New Jersey. As a result, state officials argued their proposal constituted a threat to the top-level staff and other resources that might be allocated to USFWS to support wetland permitting responsibilities. State officials continue to believe that the Fish and Wildlife Service turned assumption into a turf-war and used its influence with the EDF and Sierra Club to oppose New Jersey assumption.

Although environmental issue groups initially supported New Jersey's assumption of wetlands permitting and the consolidation of those activities, the USFWS's opposition resulted in an almost immediate loss of environmental support. One of the primary assumptions held by many environmental groups was that state responsibility for consolidated permitting assumption would protect wetlands. The intervention by the Fish and Wildlife Service undoubtedly led some environmental groups to attempt to influence then-Governor James Florio, who was politically vulnerable and seeking reelection, to delay or withdraw the New Jersey application. Florio, who was ultimately defeated for reelection in 1993 by Whitman, deferred the application submission until after the election, thereby assuaging environmental groups. The final irony of this drama comes after Florio's defeat, when several environmental groups, apparently realizing they would not get a better deal with the incoming Republican governor, contacted the NJDNR and asked "what can we do to help you with assumption?"

How Can the EPA Improve Section 404 Assumption?

Not surprisingly, New Jersey officials asserted that the primary way to improve the state assumption process is for federal regulators to decide that they support assumption. The federal agencies involved in the New Jersey assumption were uncoordinated, and New Jersey was often caught between federal agency battles. A New Jersey Division of Water official observed that "[w]e are already fighting against economic and special interest groups in the state; why do we have to watch the federal agencies fight as well?" Even while the EPA and Bush and Clinton administrations urged state government to pursue assumption of wetlands regulation, other federal agencies tried to derail state assumption or to persuade states to pursue alternatives that preserved the existing roles of federal agencies in wetlands regulation. Attempts by the Corps of Engineers and the Fish and Wildlife service to block assumption or get New Jersey to pursue the statewide programmatic general permit illustrate how federal agencies worked against each other. And, some alternatives proffered by the federal agencies are politically untenable in the states. For states with more extensive wetlands regulations, the SPGP is not likely to be helpful. For example, in the case of New Jersey, the state permit did not fulfill the mandate of the state legislation, and did not adequately cover the enforcement provisions of state regulations.

Funding and Political Vulnerability

Because New Jersey had already funded its program and set up an infrastructure, the state was not eligible for most wetlands program grants awarded by the EPA. The only external funding the state received in preparing for its assumption of the 404 program was a section 103 grant for $25,000 to design a computer linkage between the New Jersey Department of Natural Resources and the Pinelands area enforcement zone, which had its own data bases and computer system.

Funding of the NJDEP's wetland regulation program is obtained from revenues generated by the permit program. For the first two years of the state program, the general assembly funded the program. It has since become self-supporting. The permit fee process allows the New Jersey DEP to maintain a high degree of functional independence. The program has been financially independent since 1989. Operating costs in 1988–1989 and 1989–1990 were approximately $1.1 million for all of the state's wetlands program. The program brought in $3.3 million in 1988–1989 and $4.2 million in fees during 1989–1990. Any revenue surplus goes into the New Jersey general fund and is not dedicated to the NJDEP's general expenses or to wetlands protection specifically.

Although the state charges a fee for its general permit to generate revenue, New Jersey Governor Whitman indicated her belief during her 1993 campaign that the fees were a hidden tax. She contended that the program should be funded through general revenues rather than from a permit fee. However, reliance on general revenues shifts the burden of paying of permitting away from the developer and to the general taxpayer. One NJDNR official indicated that the independent funding allows the freshwater wetlands program to work with less fear of legislative oversight or constraints on its budget. As a result, if funding is returned to the general appropriation bill, the state legislature and governor will be better positioned to exert political influence on the program.

Fears that the change from a dedicated permit-fee to a general fund appropriation will bring more political influence to bear on wetland regulation may be overstated. Two New Jersey officials observed that even if funding for the program returned to the general appropriation bill, it will still be preserved because of ongoing EPA oversight. A state species protection official noted that attempts by Michigan's governor, John Englar, to weaken that state's section 404 permit program resulted in the EPA indicating it would reassume section 404 authority if the consolidated permit program were underfunded or otherwise weakened. In effect, the potential adverse publicity for state officials from such an attempt seemingly preempts any serious debilitation of the 404 program. And, the EPA had previously indicated its willingness to defend the integrity of the assumed program in Michigan, by canceling the MOA with a state that slashed funding of the program to a level that rendered it ineffective.

Workloads

According to New Jersey officials, their workload remains essentially unchanged since assumption. Because of the nature of the New Jersey law, virtually every USACE/EPA permit application is processed by the state. The redundancy of the state and federal programs meant that New Jersey was already on the site for most wetland permit decisions. The EPA workload should increase substantially following state assumption, because the EPA must conduct periodic review of the New Jersey program. At the same time, the Fish and Wildlife Service has virtually withdrawn from wetlands permitting in New Jersey, despite the increased opportunities for comment and input on more permits under the assumed program.

The Perception of Oversight

A senior state regulator in New Jersey maintained that "whenever EPA oversight catches an error or omission by the state program, they treat it like some sort of sin." In fact, one of the primary fears voiced about state assumption, according to both environmental groups and development interests was that local political influences would prevail in permitting decisions. New Jersey officials are optimistic that this perception will change as builders and environmental groups realize that the state's decisions are still subject to federal oversight. Presumably, this belief rests on the assumption that, because the EPA maintains oversight of the New Jersey program, concerns over undue political influence will cause close scrutiny. Overly blatant politicization without technical support could lead the EPA to rescind the state's assumption of permitting authority, as we discussed earlier in this chapter.

One positive benefit that both state and federal officials noted was the reduction in delays caused by individuals who use the bifurcated state/federal permit system to seek favorable regulation. Put simply, the assumption of the 404 program prevents individuals from playing federal and state authorities against each other. Instead, all permitting decisions are made within the state, with veto power over approvals retained by federal regulators. Under split jurisdiction between state and federal regulators, the conflicts between different delineations and levels of tolerance of the laws often led to delay in permitting.

New Jersey in Summary

It is too early to assess the effective improvement of the implementation of wetland regulation and protection under the New Jersey program. However, there are lessons about the process of implementing assumption that stand in stark contrast to the Michigan experience. The characterization of New Jersey's experience as "how things are not done" was advanced by an interview subject; however, it is an accurate assessment that reflects our evaluation of the New Jersey experience.

New Jersey moved forward with assumption at the behest of an incumbent, second-term governor who had a strong commitment to the wetland issue, and who was willing to use political muscle to advance assumption of federal authority. Because the initiative to take on section 404 necessarily moves bottom-up, from the states to the federal level, such support is important. But it is not sufficient to grease the skids of implementation. Kean's legislation did not recognize the temporal reality of assumption, despite the supposed knowledge New Jersey officials professed of the Michigan experience. And, enthusiasm for Governor Kean's proposal, as well as his influence, was confined to his own state legislature and bureaucracy. The major federal agencies involved in section 404 did not share the common goal of seeing New Jersey take over section 404. We cannot emphasize enough the role of bureaucratic conflict between state and federal regulators in rendering the New Jersey experience unpleasant.

It is important to note that New Jersey's assumption was not seriously delayed by the political resistence to the program from the FWS and the Corps of Engineers. Instead, it was the learning curve on implementing assumption—the ignorance of New Jersey about what assumption entailed—that created much of the frustration in this process. Once New Jersey had completed a correct and complete application, the process of moving section 404 to the state was relatively smooth, and in fact moved along as quickly as in Michigan

Concluding Thoughts, Mixed Signals

Our examination of the two states that have assumed section 404 reveals that assumption can be political and frustrating, but the process also is ultimately rewarding, at least for state regulators. Michigan and New Jersey state officials uniformly indicated a high degree of satisfaction with their respective state programs. And, both states' regulators repeatedly touted the superiority of the state-administered programs. Whatever the problems involved in their initial assumption of consolidated permitting under section 404, state regulators in both New Jersey and Michigan perceive (or obtained, in the case of Michigan) longterm benefits from being the primary locus for state wetlands regulation *vis-a-vis* approving development proposals.

The other consideration in encouraging states to assume section 404 permitting authority is the extent that the assumption process is politically charged. For example, according to a senior federal water official who was involved with assumption in the 1970s and 1980s at the Michigan Department of Natural Resources, the assumption process in that state went smoothly because the EPA was anxious for some state to assume section 404 authority. The EPA viewed Michigan as the most likely candidate, and no significant opposition existed at the state level, although the official recalled "minor" nitpicking over the memorandum of agreement. Even if reflections about the assumption process in Michigan are clouded by time and the program's success, the perceived longterm value of state consolidation of wetlands regulation seems to have made it worth tackling the initial political and administrative obstacles.

Because the assumption experience was so recent, the politics surrounding the New Jersey experience are still fresh in the memories of state and Federal officials. To a large extent, the temporal proximity of those experiences probably are more relevant to what states may experience in the future. When multiple agencies are involved in the implementation of a policy, turf battles and conflicts concerning jurisdiction are almost inevitable, especially if the involved agencies have divergent missions. However, the conflicts in implementation are compounded by changes in the scope of agency involvement that threaten the missions and funding of individual agencies. As states move to assume functional authority over federal programs such as section 404, or have such functional control thrust upon them via federal mandates, the federal agencies that must sanction state assumption will assess the impact of assumption based on the agency's fiscal and political needs.

States that assume section 404 authority can appear to be a real and immediate threat to the fiscal security and the missions of federal agencies such as the Fish and Wildlife Service, especially amid the expected insecurities in the current era of constrained budgets, increasing demand for government-provided goods and services, and efforts in the federal executive branch and legislature to downsize the national government. For special interests seeking to influence policy content or outputs, the existence of a policy domain that is fractured among disagreeing agencies and across levels of government presents an opportunity to exercise substantial leverage. However, it also impedes the resolution of policy differences, and can lead to policy compromises that are to the benefit of selected interests rather than the public good, and which also serves as barriers to implementation.

If we consider the New Jersey and Michigan assumption implementations through a wider lens, then the process has many of the characteristics associated with successful implementation processes. The goal, a transition from federal to state authority, is clearly defined. All of the possible agency actors who come into contact with the target of policy are involved in the reformulation of the assumed program, and formal avenues exist for communication of opinions and objections. The process is not driven from the top down. Instead, as we saw in both New Jersey and Michigan, the state takes the initiative to alter the policy design. And, the lead agency in the process, the Environmental Protection Agency, has a record of acting in a cooperative and professional fashion in helping states take over these programs.

5

Two Divergent Paths:
Florida and Maryland

The Stone-Age politicians want to screw up north Florida the way
they screwed up south Florida. Assumption? Don't do it unless you
have to.

Florida Department of Environmental
Protection Official

The narrative in the previous chapter indicated that the assumption process is an involved and drawn-out process that has left an indelible impression on both of the states where it was attempted. In Michigan, the process proved to be ultimately rewarding, while in New Jersey the delays and impediments to implementing assumption were frustrating to state officials. Implementation of assumption lays bare the competing interests in the environmental regulation community. The experiences of Michigan and New Jersey left us with another question to be answered: What are the perceptions and evaluations of section 404 assumption in states that are seriously considering assumption, but have not gone through the process?

Section 404 assumption is voluntary, and relies on a strong initiative from the bottom of the regulatory system—the state—to proceed with devolution. The decision to proceed with implementing assumption is dependent on the needs and desires of state officials and political actors. Those officials look to the institutional memory that surrounds assumption of the program, in order to help structure the costs and benefits associated with assumption. In this chapter, we examine two states that have been involved in wetland regulation for several years: Florida and Maryland. Both states have strong freshwater wetland laws, and both considered assumption of the section 404 program for several years. Recently, however, these two states diverged in their formulation of new wetlands regulation. In 1994 Maryland was vigorously pursuing state assumption of the 404 program, while Florida was no longer considering assumption, and instead was turning to other options to improve wetlands protection and permitting in the Sunshine State.

Florida

To understand the dynamics of assumption in Florida, it is useful to explore the background of wetlands regulation in the state. In the two states we have already studied, both had established, unified state-level programs for the regulation of wetland resources. In Florida, we see an additional complication to the structure of regulatory authority for wetlands. Until 1994, two state agencies regulated different aspects of state wetlands policy. The state Water Management Districts (WMDs) regulated flood control, runoff, and consumptive use of the state waters of Florida; the state is divided among five regional districts. Another agency, the Florida Department of Environmental Regulation (FDER) regulated water quality and discharge-and-fill programs similar to the federal section 404 program (see also Swanson and Stoutamire, n.d.). Individuals performing work in areas containing wetlands often found that they had to make two permitting stops at the state level, in addition to obtaining their federal section 404 permit and the section 401 water quality certificate. In addition, the water management districts regulate a whole other classification of wetland, the isolated wetland, which are not covered by the mandate of the Florida Department of Environmental Protection (FDEP). Presumably, this discrepancy will be eliminated in the future. The new uniform wetlands delineation passed by the legislature in 1994 incorporates isolated wetlands into a uniform methodology for all state agencies. However, discrepancies remain between state and federal delineation methodologies, and these differences represent a barrier to consolidated permitting and state assumption of federal authority.

Florida first began considering consolidated wetlands permitting in the late 1980s. Mark Latch, then administrator of the Florida Department of Environmental Protection, traveled to Michigan in 1988 and discussed assumption with the Michigan Department of Natural Resources staff. There were no gubernatorial initiatives from Governors Graham, Martinez, or Chiles on this issue. Instead, the impetus to examine consolidation started with the state environmental agency and its former director, Carol Browner, who left Florida's DEP in 1993 to become EPA administrator in the Clinton administration.

In October 1991, the chairmen of the Florida Senate and House Committees on Natural Resources wrote a joint letter to then EPA Administrator William K. Reilly, asking for information on state assumption of the 404 dredge and fill permitting program. The two committee chairs, Senator George Kirkpatrick and Representative Hurley Rudd, also asked the EPA to evaluate the impact of proposed mergers or re-delegation of the state permitting authorities on assumption of federal 404.

The EPA responded in a December 1991 letter from George Tidwell, EPA region 4 administrator. Tidwell's response indicated that assumption by the water management districts, the Department of Environmental Regulation, or a combination of the two programs did not present a legal problem under the definition of "state agencies." The EPA staff analysis indicated the only condition for a state agency to assume section 404 was that it must meet all "substantive requirements" of the Clean Water Act.

In effect, for the Florida Department of Environmental Regulation and the Water Management Districts to share the responsibility for 404 assumption, they would have to submit one proposal for one program which clearly delineated the responsibilities of each agency, and how the agencies would coordinate implementation. The directors of all involved agencies would have to be party to the memorandum of agreement with the EPA and the Corps of Engineers. If any one agency failed to meet the requirements, the entire program would be withdrawn. An alternative course of action would be for one agency to assume 404 authority and then delegate certain responsibilities to another agency. The nature of the delegation would have to be described clearly in the memorandum of agreement. EPA oversight would fall on the assuming state agency, which would then be held accountable for all actions under the auspices of the state.

The initial state proposal to assume a partial 404 program was not permissible under the Clean Water Act. The EPA report noted a variety of issues to be addressed for section 404 assumption by Florida. Principal among these:

- The state's definition and delineation of wetlands would have to be broadened to federal delineation.

- The current state permit program issues 20–25 year permits, where Corps of Engineers/EPA limits state 404 programs to 5-year permits; Florida would have to shorten the length of state permits.

- The state would have to drop the 90-day default permit issue, and allow for federal review and comment period of at least 90 days.

- State public comment period and hearings provisions would need to be modified (this provision is unclear as to the precise nature of the problem).

In an effort to streamline the permitting process, the WMDs and the FDER informally brokered an agreement to allow for limited one-stop permitting at the state level. In late 1992, the WMDs began to process state water quality permits for certain projects in areas where they usually had more permit applications, while the FDER began to process WMD permits in areas where they had more permit requests. This was the beginning of "one-stop shopping" in terms of Florida's wetland regulation. Subsequently, the state legislature formalized this arrangement by merging the WMDs permitting authority with the FDER and the Department of Natural Resources to create a new Florida Department of Environmental Protection (FDEP). The formation of this agency action is in line with the recent history of state program streamlining in Florida.

During the 1993 legislative session, the legislature authorized the merger of state permitting under WMDs and FDER into a combined Florida Department of Environmental Protection. The state consolidated state permitting, and included language encouraging 404 permit assumption or the pursuit of a State Program General Permit (SPGP), which allows the state to jointly administer the USACE 404 program. This legislative endorsement represents the high-water mark for efforts in Florida at section 404 assumption. Through the balance of the decade the state political climate has become inhospitable to increased government activism.

Where Assumption Stands

Assumption of the 404 program by Florida is dead for the near-term (probably the next three to five years). In 1994 Florida officials decided not to pursue assumption of the section 404 permit program for the near future. A variety of state, agency, and federal factors have played into the decision to not pursue 404. Instead, the state is actively pursuing a state programmatic general permit as an extension of their existing effort to streamline the state permitting system. The EPA and the state water management districts and the DEP are continuing a pilot project funded under the EPA's Wetlands Protection State Development Grant program. This project will allow the state to develop a common mechanism for sharing information about permit applications, thereby expediting decisionmaking, compliance, and enforcement.

The effort to develop a common information system and permitting program may be for naught. It is commonly believed that the SPGP option is not politically feasible. The Republican political successes of the mid-1990s, winning control of first the state senate and then the state house, indicate that an assumption bill is not likely to be forthcoming. The state is not expanding its wetland regulation operation, but is instead cutting positions. Since 1994, the DEP has voluntarily eliminated numerous positions in its wetlands office through budget cuts or reassignment, leading several employees to make public their belief that wetland protection in Florida is a "doomed enterprise" (Ritchie, 1997). The demise of the wetland office was underscored by the cut of 17 additional positions by the legislature in 1997. The political will and desire is not present in the legislature or among agency leaders at the DEP to increase the state/federal relationship in regulating wetlands, let alone having the state assume federal authority for wetlands protection

Pursuing the SPGP is still an attractive option until the regulatory and political problems with full assumption are resolved. However, that option also faces an uncertain political future. The legislation had the general approval of the chairs of both the state House and Senate Natural Resources Committees in the early 1990s, but the change in party control has eliminated the strong leadership for the SPGP option in the legislature. The attempt to create a general state permit has also encountered resistance from development and building interests in the state, and from the National Wildlife Federation (NWF). A source at the Florida Department of Environmental Protection indicated that the NWF does not like anything that FDEP does, so resistance is expected on all initiatives.

Administrators and legislative sources readily agree that Florida will not have a fully-consolidated wetlands permit program prior to the twenty-first century. In the short run, there are too many negatives related to the assumption process, and there is little immediate indication that the congress is prepared to address those problems. One FDEP official described 404 assumption as being like "shooting at a moving target," especially until the Clean Water Act reauthorization is completed. As a result, state water regulators assumed a wait-and-see approach to wetlands consolidation, rather than face what they perceive to be the inevitable application problems that hindered New Jersey assumption (see chapter 4).

The primary problem with assumption or creating and SPGP for Florida is determining the "line" of activity or tolerance permitting agencies must draw. A state official indicated that there is a *de facto* line for wetlands-use enforcement that USACE has drawn, but it differs from the "perfect" line to which the Corps of Engineers and the EPA hold permitting states entities. This reflects the argument made by New Jersey regulators when recalling their assumption experience. The problem in crafting state legislation involves determining what activities will be acceptable to the Corps of Engineers, the EPA, and the Fish and Wildlife Service, as well as to the legislature and the governor. The level of state legislative uncertainty is heightened by the dramatic growth of Republican legislative strength in the state. The state agency responded to the arguments of developers and environmental groups opposed to the general permit by noting that the consolidated state program will streamline the permitting process. For Florida, the USFWS and EPA and interest groups such as EDF have not shown active opposition to state initiatives, although this may not be the case if section 404 assumption is pursued.

All indications from the state legislature were that the SPGP was not a legislative priority, and that the initiative probably would not attain priority status for some time. The staff of the House and Senate Natural Resources committees were of the opinion that the wetlands SPGP legislation would not pass during the 1994 session, and subsequent efforts to move this legislation met with no success. The 1994 Florida Senate version contained a controversial provision regarding legislative approval of the regulations drafted by the Florida Department of Environmental Protection, and the Democratic governor opposed this provision, contending that it usurped the prerogatives of the executive. Although the legislature failed to pass the enabling legislation for the SPGP, on May 5, 1994, the legislature passed a unified wetland delineation bill. The new wetlands rules reconciled the differences between delineation rules of the various state agencies. The new delineation does not expand the scope of wetlands beyond that existing under the culmination of all previous delineation rules. Some existing delineation would have classified any currently delineated wetland to be a wetland under the new rules (Florida House of Representatives, 1994a). Nevertheless, changes in the state definition of wetlands and state methodologies for identifying wetlands are necessary to move forward with a consolidated federal/state permit program.

The delineation of wetlands under Florida law is likely to move closer to the Corps of Engineers delineation. To the extent this happens, the main points of contention in wetland regulation are likely to be clarified once this legislation goes into force. Similarly, the consolidation of the state water management district permit with the Department of Environmental Regulation wetlands-use permit should expedite the permitting process. On the other hand, further changes in the Florida's definition of wetlands and the state's methodology for identifying wetlands will still be necessary before permit consolidation can occur.

Problems with Assumption

Florida administrators noted a variety of problems with the 404 assumption program that make assumption unattractive to the state. Florida wetland regulations allow the state to issue permits for periods as long as 25 years. Under section 404, the USACE also issues long-term permits, but a state-assumed consolidated permit program permit is limited to a period of five years by the rules governing state-assumed 404 programs. For Florida officials, these constraints are problematic for two reasons. First, the state would be effectively curtailing its authority and abrogating much final authority to the federal regulators. The current state permits are issued for periods of up to 20 years, much like the 404 permits issued by USACE under 404. Second, short-term permits are not conducive to effective long-range planning or development. For example, the large-scale projects of the Disney Corporation require longer-term permits to accommodate their developments outside of Orlando.

Florida officials contend that another problem with the process is that section 404 assumption is an "all-or-nothing" proposition. Either a state takes over the entire program in all assumable waters or assumes none of the program. In the opinion of Florida regulators, the transition program under section 404 is impossible, since on the day that assumption becomes official, "the semis role up with every permit and document Corps has considered, is considering, or will consider in your state," according to one official. The transfer of data and workload is immediate. Florida regulators contend that the state should be allowed to phase in 404 assumption, arguing immediate transition is not good for the assuming party or for the regulated community. The EPA Region 4 officials have contradicted this characterization of assumption transition, claiming that the metaphor of truckloads of paperwork is inaccurate. However, the perception of a bad transition carries as much or more weight among Florida officials than the reality of the two assumption experiences.

The state deferred assumption of section 404 authority and decided to "do consolidation right," rather than confront the myriad of organizational and political headaches that other states have encountered. This approach has been supported by public interest groups, and by environmental groups such as Partners for a Better Florida.

Another problem the Florida DEP encountered is convincing interest groups and legislators to consider all aspects of assumption. Now that state consolidation is nearly complete, legislators and constituents are realizing that they have only covered two-thirds of the process, and that they need to address state/federal consolidation. State agency officials apparently encounter high levels of political myopia when attempting to convince state legislators how to formulate sensible, efficient water policy.

"The Problem with Federal Regulators"

The state regulators we spoke with in 1994 contended that they had not enjoyed a great deal of cooperation from regional EPA regulators. For example, the state letter requesting information and advice on wetlands assumption and consolidation that was sent by the legislature was not replied to until three months later, when correspondence arrived from EPA region 4 in Atlanta. State administrators indicted that they received no cooperation from region 4 on the issue of assumption. They are left with the perception that the EPA regional office does not seem committed to assumption, and that EPA will not dedicate the resources to expediting the assumption process. When Florida decided to pursue assumption as one potential avenue for improving wetlands regulation, they received $260,000 in federal development grants for the joint study of assumption with the EPA. Of this, over $60,000 went unspent because the EPA regional office would not commit time or personnel resources to the endeavor. One Florida official argued that the "EPA should have committed at least half of an attorney, half of a permitting expert, and part of another staffer to this question . . . We sent a assumption proposal up to them for review over a year ago, and we have never heard back from them." While the perspective is biased toward the state, the presence of substantial unspent funds lends credence to the state official's argument. By comparison, the Corps of Engineers was enthusiastic about actively pursuing the state SPGP, and has been cooperative on assumption matters. The USACE and Florida are operating a trial joint permit processing program in the Jacksonville area as a precursor to the full SPGP. As in the New Jersey case, there is a degree of confusion between federal agencies and across levels of those agencies concerning the direction and importance of 404 assumption.

Delineation Problems

There are problems with state assumption of 404 that relate to wetlands delineation. In order to assume the federal 404 program, a state must have a definition of wetlands which is at least as stringent as the federal definition. In the next legislative session, the Florida DEP will include 404 guidelines and amendments to delineation in its legislation, while leaving explicit assumption legislation out of their proposal. If the state will not change the 404 delineation, it will be impossible to achieve complete permit consolidation. Problems of delineation focus on the status of isolated wetlands and on the treatment of pine flatwoods in Collier County. According to federal regulators, the pine flatwoods are considered wetlands because they sustain standing water for extended periods after heavy rain, and support vegetation typical of wetlands. The state excludes pine flatwoods from their wetland delineation because the species of pine growing in these flatwoods cannot thrive in areas that have longterm standing water or are often immersed. Regulating these lands creates potential problems with silviculture, timber interests, and builders.

Another problem under the regulations governing 404, as noted previously, is that categories of wetlands exist that state programs cannot assume. Those phase I wetlands constitute approximately 60 percent of all wetlands in Florida, and include much of the Everglades. For Florida regulators, the assumption of section 404 would not allow the state to obtain full statutory authority over the most important waters in Florida's fragile ecosystem. Relative to the effort required to obtain assumption, the extent of authority the state derives from assumption is relatively small.

Interim Solution: Statewide Programmatic General Permits

Given problems of delineation and assumption, Florida is pursuing the state programmatic general permit as an alternative to the politically untenable assumption of 404. In particular, the SPGP precludes many of the problems with assumption. The problems of time span (five-year versus 25-year permits) and partial jurisdictions are avoided, and the state is still able to have input on all permitting decisions and have a streamlined process.

A particular advantage of the SPGP involves the role of the Fish and Wildlife Service in enforcing laws governing endangered plants and animals and the elevation process. Under a SPGP, the USFWS district office is able to authorize or dispute a "taking" at the district level, thereby localizing the decision process (see chapter 3). However, under 404 assumption, any "taking" has to be elevated to EPA headquarters in Washington, as well as to the USFWS headquarters, thereby adding multiple layers of bureaucracy and delaying the permit process. Because regulatory "takings" are more common in Florida than in most other states, elevation events would occur often under an assumed 404 program, and result in increased bureaucratic delay. Not assuming section 404 allows the state to retain the more convenient level of appeals for the regulated public in takings disputes, an unexpected positive consequence of not streamlining. This action also maintains the speed of a more localized permit process.

The Endangered Species Misperception

Florida has had little formal resistance to permit consolidation or assumption from organized environmental or construction interests. Historically, the state has been a leader in terms of land-use and water regulation. The strong program already in place preempts most resistance to assumption or the use of an SPGP. One of the principal misconceptions that exist under the assumption process is that the USFWS will lose enforcement under an assumed program; this concern was also voiced in New Jersey. In fact, the EPA is positioned under its oversight mechanism to rescind any permit the state issues. Florida administrators found it ironic that environmental groups "emphasized the good job that the Corps of Engineers did in enforcement, but that these same groups [do not] trust the Federal agencies to oversee a state-run program."

The Information Problem

Much of the problem faced by Florida in pursuing any sort of permitting reform arises from communication and information difficulties. Most legislators do not realize the complicated issues surrounding assumption; they are confronted with competing demands from constituents, and also by the presence of a powerful builders and development lobby. This problem is further exacerbated by the rapid degree of political turnover in the legislature, which is diminishing institutional memory. Many senior members from both parties have departed office in the last five years, either due to defeat or attaining higher office; and, other senior members are threatened by the impending imposition of a term-limit law. Most actors in the political drama of Florida find themselves having to reinvent contacts and recreate knowledge bases within the legislature. The FDEP administrators see the education of legislators and interest groups as their primary role in helping design assumption strategies. Career state regulators argued that the legislature needs a clear understanding of the impact of full assumption versus SPGP or some other hybrid program on Florida's environment and on efficiency in government. Because the state has focused exclusively on the streamlining of the state program while ignoring the federal dimension, many of the education efforts undertaken for state permit consolidation will have to be repeated in the next decade for federal-state consolidation.

Florida's growth constitutes another problem. The development problems of South Florida may be repeated in North Florida, placing added pressure on water resources. The key for state policymakers, in their mind, is to stay out ahead of the development curve. Large projects—Walt Disney World is a good example—have very long term impacts which are not served by a five-year permit. The state has to be positioned to engage in activity which encourages longterm planning and allows the state to make longterm decisions. The next step, once the state SPGP is negotiated and approved, is to return to the legislature and fix the delineation problems. Returning to the observations of a senior Florida official, "[Florida needs] to negotiate an SPGP involving everything we can get." Of greatest importance is that Florida follow an orderly progression, and not jump in too quickly. As one Florida official wryly observed, "New Jersey wasn't ready, and they got in over their heads. It caused problems."

Maryland

The state of Maryland has a long history of wetland protection and regulation. Over 20 years ago, the state passed legislation governing the use and protection of tidal wetlands. The state has assumed the section 402 National Pollution Discharge Elimination System (NPDES) program, and also issues a state water quality certificate under section 401 of the Clean Water Act. In January 1991 the state water division began operation of wetland regulation under a state programmatic general permit. In 1995 the state started developing an application for full section 404 assumption. However, the legislation necessary to proceed with the application was rejected by the state legislature, which effectively derailed the section 404 initiative in Maryland. The state does operate under a state programmatic general permit, issued in 1991, and the renewal of that permit in 1996 was subsequently followed by the suspension of several nationwide permits in Maryland, which effectively reduced the presence of the Corps of Engineers in many permitting decisions (U.S. Army, 1997; Zawotski, 1997). And there is still enthusiasm in certain sectors of the state environmental community for complete state assumption of section 404 authority.

The Assumption Strategy

The impetus to assume section 404 comes from language in the Non-Tidal Wetland Act (1989). This legislation, in extending state regulation of freshwater wetlands, also directed the Maryland Department of Natural Resources (MdDNR) to investigate assumption of the 404 program. This legislation, passed with the enthusiastic support of Governor William Donald Schaefer, represented the governor's first major environmental legislative victory. The governor was subsequently one of the most ardent supporters of state assumption of section 404. Although much of his enthusiasm no doubt derived from his support of wetlands protection, part of the impetus is highly pragmatic. Schaefer is an opponent of duplicate federal or state programs, and wants to streamline needlessly burdensome regulatory practices. The governor stated that he wants assumption completed before the end of his term in 1995. This particular desire did not come to pass.

The road to assumption has been a rocky one for Maryland. To a certain extent the state "jumped into" assumption without knowing what they were getting into, thereby following the lead of New Jersey. According to a non-tidal wetlands regulator at the Maryland Department of Natural Resources (DNR), the initial examination of assumption indicated that Maryland was not ready for assumption. And, the incumbent governor who was pushing for increased wetlands protection was less hurried about assumption than was New Jersey Governor Kean. Rather than jumping into the assumption process as New Jersey did in 1987, Maryland instead applied for a state programmatic general permit, which went into force in 1991.

Maryland pursued assumption of section 404 and the SPGP due to dissatisfaction in state agencies, the governor's office, and among the regulated public with the USACE implementation of their regulatory mandate under section 404. Until the granting of the SPGP, the state attempted to use their section 401 water quality certificate to compensate for lax or inconsistent USACE permitting. The Maryland DNR "stretched to the legal limits" the ability to regulate wetlands through section 401; any further state influence on wetlands protection would require 404 assumption, at the very least. In particular, state regulators found USACE's section 404 implementation to be inadequate for protecting the Chesapeake Bay.

The arbitrary nature of USACE implementation of section 404 is a theme encountered throughout this study. In Maryland, however, the problem with section 404 enforcement cannot be blamed on implementation by multiple district offices because all of Maryland is under the Baltimore district. Therefore, inconsistencies cannot be blamed on the different regulatory style of district engineers, as was the case in New Jersey. Instead, the problem with permitting is one of delineation. USACE has been inconsistent in classifying projects under general or individual permits, which is a problem encountered in many other states. Even under the SPGP, in place since 1991, the state battled USACE over the appropriate use of individual permits. One Maryland regulator observed that "the Corps keeps stamping everything as nationwide and sending it out." The Corps of Engineers appeared to be having a hard time letting go of its 404 responsibility in Maryland.

Another administrator thinks that the problem in Maryland stems from the decentralized philosophy of the USACE's bureaucracy. District engineers serve three-year appointments, and then move on to their next assignment. For field implementors at the Corps of Engineers there is little incentive to change their style or procedures, because if any implementation conflicts with a district engineer arise, they can be stretched out until a new district engineer is appointed. Under such conditions enforcing real change within USACE is difficult.

Although the Corps of Engineers has not opposed the state's 404 assumption plan, USACE could serve as an impediment similar to the role filled by the New York district office during the New Jersey assumption process. Because the size of USACE district budgets is determined by the number of permits they process, those offices can be expected to respond like other bureaucracies by trying to protect their administrative and budgetary turf through resisting assumption. Conversely, it is possible USACE may be engaging in more rigorous implementation of 404 guidelines to forestall the need for state assumption. One state official noted that USACE administration and district engineers "have good intentions; the staff is the problem."

U.S. Fish and Wildlife Service

State implementors indicated that the USFWS is not very active in the section 404 program in Maryland, either before or since the state programmatic general permit went into effect. The USFWS is notified with every public notice of a permit application. The only times they are actively involved is when state or USACE authorities explicitly ask for USFWS involvement.

The state assumption plan is opposed by many officials at the USFWS. Although the service rarely involves itself in Maryland permit decisions, officials at the service believes species protection will suffer under state jurisdiction; the fact that Maryland is in the same USFWS region as New Jersey underscores the importance of these observations. Many of the individuals that were dealt with by New Jersey in their assumption effort will also be administratively active in the Maryland case. While a senior Maryland environmental regulator we talked to does not believe they will encounter resistance from the regional office, he did note the tactics used by the Brunswick section office during the New Jersey assumption.

The reasons for Fish and Wildlife Service resistance to state assumption are driven by the same factors noted in New Jersey and Michigan: Loss of budget and staff resources; and fear that federal responsibilities under the USFWS's mandate will not be executed. The first reason is a logical response for any bureaucracy. When the mission of an agency is threatened or significantly altered, the intuitive response of individuals who are dependant on the agency is to protect the agency and oppose change. Changes in mission lead to reallocation of financial and personnel resources, or to cuts in the program. The assumption by a state of a complex, expensive program such as 404 could impair the budgetary security of several federal offices in the state.

The second concern, loss of federal protection such as the Endangered Species Act, is countered by Maryland officials who contend that this argument is easily addressed by the conditions that prevail under state assumption:

- Maryland law governing species and habitat is stricter than the federal Endangered Species Act. The state law has a longer list of protected species, thereby increasing the number of species factors considered in making permitting decisions.

- Because the state reviews all permit applications, including those for activities previously covered by nationwide and general permits—and therefore not subject to extensive review or public comment under USACE implementation— the state subjects more applications to the scrutiny of an endangered species law than were previously under Corps implementation.

- In relation to the previous point, USFWS retains the right of comment on all permit applications under assumption. State assumption actually expands the range of applications and activities subject to USFWS comment.

- Phase I waters will continue to be subject to section 10 regulation and therefore will also be subject to section 404 regulation by the Corps of Engineers as well as all federal endangered species laws.

- The state will be able to place more personnel in the field to regulate endangered species provisions of the broader state law.

One cannot be certain that state personnel will better able to identify and protect endangered species than will Fish and Wildlife Service personnel. However, given the universal disdain expressed
towards the USFWS in Maryland and elsewhere towards the
USACE, especially in EPA regions 4 and 7 (see EPA, 1990), state
implementors will be hard-pressed to give less consideration to
endangered species criteria than USACE currently does in many
jurisdictions.

Interest Groups

Environmental groups have expressed firm opposition to the state's
plan to assume section 404. On the other hand, the entire regulated
community, most legislators, and the governor firmly support assumption. The concerns of environmental groups mirror those of the
Fish and Wildlife Service, which fears the disappearance of federal
mechanisms protecting the resource after assumption. These groups
doubt Maryland's ability to step in and effectively maintain comparable levels of enforcement, and question the adequacy of Maryland's regulatory structure to protect the resource. One activist
described the federal mechanism as allowing "two bites" at permitting—one federal, the other at the state level.

Members of the regulated community, on the other hand, are
concerned with the inconsistent and arbitrary nature of USACE
wetlands permitting decisions. While state regulations may be more
strict, they will also be more predictable. This stance reflects the traditional attitude of many industries toward state regulation. If the
public sector is going to regulate an activity, the industry wants
clear, specific regulations and consistent implementation and enforcement in order to make the regulatory process more predictable
for planning and compensation for regulatory costs.

Advantages to State Assumption in Maryland

Maryland water regulators contend that there are several advantages for the environment and the regulated public to state assumption of the 404 program. The state statute and regulations cover a
greater variety of activities than the federal 404 regulations. Activities normally covered by 404 nationwide permits are examined on a
case-by-case basis. Such a permitting process reduces the likelihood

of mistakenly granting a permit to a project that might require remediation or mitigation. Also, the state's own endangered species act is extended into decisions where federal laws were not rigorously enforced, mirroring an argument advanced in New Jersey.

The greater detail of the state permitting program decreases the latitude available to field-level personnel. Mazmanian and Sabatier (1981) note that ensuring a successful implementation from the top-down is based in part on clarity of statutes and regulations. Precautions such as these leave little discretion for field staff, and help reduce the arbitrary or random elements of implementation. This level of detail is especially welcomed by Maryland implementors, who are able to lean on a detailed law and regulation package to relieve themselves from external political influence by state lawmakers. One administrator observed:

> "I am glad the law and regulations are detailed. When we get some legislator coming in here asking for favors, we can pull out the regs and say 'here is the law. What you want is illegal; we can't do it.' I can't tell you how often [Maryland U.S. Senators] Mikulski or Sarbanes are calling Corps to get a favor done. No politician has ever figured out how to influence our permit process."

Interestingly, the entire Maryland congressional delegation supported state assumption.

Like Florida, Michigan, and New Jersey, the state is in the position to assign more staff to the field. The state can place 32 permitters and 28 enforcement officers in the field, which is substantially more personnel resources than the USACE and USFWS can make available. Placing these large numbers of state personnel to the task of permitting also frees Corps of Engineers personnel for other tasks such as enforcement and education. And, if the state really does a poor job of wetlands protection under an assumed section 404 program, then the EPA has the authority to overturn any permitting decision or discontinue the entire program, returning implementation to USACE. Preliminary evidence indicates that increased state involvement in the 404 process has improved wetlands protection. According to Maryland sources, the annual wetlands loss before the SPGP went into effect in non-phase I waters was approximately 1600 acres per year. Since the SPGP went into effect in January 1991, the loss of such freshwater wetlands has fallen of substantially to 21 acres per year.

The Assumption Process

To date, state regulatory officials have described the assumption process as "all consuming." The state has yet to submit a formal application for assumption to EPA. Although the state has sufficient legal authority under the 1989 state wetlands act to assume section 404, Maryland officials are trying to pass additional legislation governing wetlands at the state level. The failure of the assumption bill during the 1994 legislative session came about due to parliamentary tactics by senate opponents. A senior senator on the Committee on Economy and the Environment derailed the legislation, which passed the lower chamber by a 2:1 margin. The senator, described as a staunch environmental advocate by agency officials, blocked the bill from hearings or markup in committee with the help of two environmental allies. All three of those legislators retired after the legislative session. Their departure should clear the way for passage of a new wetlands bill that calls for assumption of section 404.

The state has not performed a feasibility study on assumption or submitted a formal application to the EPA. However, they are assembling a partial reapplication to submit to EPA for comment and criticism. Learning from the New Jersey experience ("a perfect example of how not to assume" according to a senior water official), the Maryland DNR is giving the EPA an opportunity to look at it "holes and all" and tell the DNR what it needs to do to assume section 404. The significant difference between the Maryland approach and that of New Jersey's is that Maryland is approaching assumption without an impending legislative deadline. Also, Maryland officials fully expect problems with their initial application. This eyes-open, patient approach to taking over the 404 permit program should help avert the tension and frustration associated with the New Jersey experience.

Maryland DNR officials have had frequent contact with the EPA headquarters as well as the EPA region 3 office in Philadelphia. The EPA has been very supportive of Maryland wetlands efforts, including assumption, at all levels, and the degree of support has increased over time. Maryland officials believe that the EPA learned the right way to do things in New Jersey, based on the problems encountered there. They expect the EPA to take greater care in protecting the assuming state from blind-side attacks. This cautious approach especially should be evident in dealings with the Fish and Wildlife Service, which probably will offer strenuous opposition to the Maryland assumption since it will come at the expense of USFWS responsibility. Again, the lessons learned from New Jersey are not lost on Maryland officials. A leading MdDNR official stated firmly that "we know [the Fish and Wildlife Service's] tactics" when opposing 404 assumption.

Summary: Lessons from Florida and Maryland

The Florida and Maryland cases resulted in different outcomes, as Maryland moved forward rapidly towards consolidated permitting while the course of Florida policy is still undetermined. Whether either state ultimately achieves full assumption is still subject to a variety of factors. The cautious approaches exercised in Florida and Maryland are in part a result of political realities. In Maryland, despite the broad support enjoyed in the regulated community and among state officials, passage into the next stage of assumption continues to be delayed by parliamentary politics; a more recent effort at passing assumption legislation failed a roll call vote in the Maryland legislature. In Florida, the adversarial legislative process that typifies Florida politics worked itself into a gridlock that resulted in little progress on several issues. It is accomplishment enough to state policymakers that the state wetlands delineation bill passed the legislature to become law.

Maryland is closer to attempting assumption than is Florida. Maryland already has an established SPGP system and is in the preapplication process for assumption. Florida has only begun pursuit of the SPGP and has postponed any assumption attempt into the twenty-first century. The Maryland political dynamic is such that assumption is a gubernatorial priority, and the next legislature should be free of any significant political obstacles. The Democratic governor of Florida, on the other hand, has been beset with a variety of non-environmental issues and confronts a legislature that has opposition partisan control. He is not positioned or disposed to push for assumption. If Republican frontrunner Jeb Bush is elected governor in 1998, the momentum for assumption may never be recovered. Further, within the Florida environmental and regulatory communities, most of the focus on wetlands regulation has been on the Everglades protection bill, conflicts with sugar cane plantations, streamlining state permitting procedures, and the consolidation of the Department of Environmental Regulation with the Water Management Districts. While the large number of wetland-related issues keep wetlands at the front of the policy agenda in Florida, it also forces section 404 assumption and its constituent delineation problems into the background. There are too many other pressing environmental issues that precede state assumption of federal wetland authority.

Another reason for caution in Maryland and Florida is the assumption experience in New Jersey. The torturous political fight for assumption revealed opposition from federal agencies. Florida and Maryland are both carefully preparing their assumption plans, and are following a methodical series of steps that may diffuse the arguments of assumption opponents. However, this "go-slow" approach also limits the commitment of the assuming states before total assumption. Florida may find an SPGP is sufficient to the regulatory needs of the resource and the community. If that is the case, the state regulatory agency can save valuable political capital in a contentious and unfriendly political environment.

Finally, the relative maturity of the Florida and Maryland programs contribute to the willingness to go slow. Florida and Maryland have been involved in wetlands regulation for decades. During our interviews we detected a high degree of impatience in the New Jersey Department of Natural Resources that partially arose from the state's recent entry into wetlands regulation. The Florida and Maryland regulators, by contrast, were far more confident about the ability of their existing programs to effectively regulate the resource. As a result, the assumption of section 404 permitting authority by these state agencies will be pursued to enhance their existing authority, rather than serving as a basis to establish regulatory preeminence.

6

Other Perspectives
on State Assumption

The Act provided very little incentive for the states to assume the program . . . the implementing regulations promulgated by EPA unnecessarily complicate the qualification and operational requirements.

U.S. Army Corps of Engineers

I n the preceding two chapters, we examined the experiences of states where assumption of section 404 was successful or still remains on the environmental regulatory agenda. The results of those analyses indicated that the assumption process is time consuming and can be fraught with political problems, although the states that assumed section 404 have found the resulting program to be satisfying. However, a number of states studied assumption of the section 404 program, only to be dissuaded from assumption for a variety of reasons. In this chapter we examine the reasons why several other states opted not to pursue assumption. In particular, we were interested in answering four specific questions:

- Why did these states decide against assumption?

- What factors were identified by state regulators as supporting or opposing assumption of the section 404 program?

- How did these states' evaluations of the assumption experience contrasted with the states that have assumed section
  404 or are still pursuing assumption?

- What suggestions did these states have to improve section
  404 assumption as a policy option and as a process?

To answer these questions, we evaluated the experience of eight
states that considered assumption of the section 404 program but
ultimately decided to forego assumption. The eight states examined
(Alabama, Kentucky, Minnesota, Nebraska, North Carolina, Oregon, South Carolina, and Wisconsin) represent a broad cross-section
of states with sufficient wetland attributes to be comparable to the
four states examined in chapters 4 and 5. Three of these states—
South Carolina, Oregon, and North Carolina—have significant
coastal waters. Two—Kentucky and Alabama—are under the partial jurisdiction of the Tennessee Valley Authority (TVA), and five
have significant amounts of non-assumable Phase I waters (Kentucky, South Carolina, North Carolina, Wisconsin, Oregon). Four
states—Kentucky, North Carolina, South Carolina, and Alabama—
are in EPA Region 4, where more wetlands permitting decisions occur than in any other EPA region (EPA, 1990), and the other four
states are in EPA regions 3, 5, and 10. Where possible, state implementors and federal regulators who conduct oversight of wetlands
regulation were interviewed. We constructed a narrative analysis of
the advantages and disadvantages to assumption. Then, from this
analysis we identified lessons for assumption based on these states'
experiences.

Oregon

In Oregon, inefficiency and the perceived ineffectiveness of the federal section 404 program led to calls for state assumption of the
dredge-and-fill program. As a part of the plan to study assumption,
the state conducted a feasibility study of section 404 assumption.
The purpose of the Oregon state study was to determine if state assumption of 404 would result in benefits by reducing regulatory
overlap; what the costs of 404 assumption were; and whether the
benefits of assumption compared favorably with the costs of as-

sumption. The initial problem identified in Oregon related to the enforcement of section 404 by the Corps of Engineers. The state found that effective, accurate delineation and identification of wetlands was lacking in many areas of potential development. This shortcoming constituted a major impediment to effective implementation and administration of the permit program. Because of the inconsistency in delineation and identification, state regulators, developers, and resource preservation advocates found themselves constantly embroiled in conflicts. An Oregon evaluator noted that "[w]etlands is a war of attrition between conservation elements seeking to arrest eradication and developers seeking to use their land." As such, the lack of clarity concerning what was a wetland and what activities are permissible in wetlands lead to confusion in the 404 process.

Policy differences and expectations undermined the achievement of effective, responsive management of the 404 program. In the early 1980s, the Corps of Engineers was forced to balance competing value sets in administration and permit decisionmaking. Conflicts often arose from local-land use plans, EPA preservation of resources, and attempts by the Corps of Engineers to apply best management practices to regulated lands. The lack of common policy goals for administering wetlands resources at various levels within agencies, as well as across different agencies, led to conflict and produced inferior, inconsistent policy outcomes.

The primary outcome of inter- and intraagency conflict in Oregon was the lack of issue resolution. There were a variety of unresolved issues surrounding section 404 at the time Oregon considered assumption, many of which echo the problems identified in Florida. The principal issues were:

- Defining wetlands;
- Determining whether 404 guidelines constituted a threshold for wetland preservation, or were simply considerations to be weighed against other factors during the public interest review;
- Deciding whether wetland damage should be avoided or simply mitigated;
- Determining how to assess the cumulative impact of regulation and degradation on wetlands systems;
- Determining how and when agencies should enforce compliance.

Unfortunately, section 404 assumption does not necessarily resolve these conflicts. The inability of the state to assume the waters where the USACE implementation complaints were most prevalent meant that the principal issues would not be resolved in many Oregon waters. Any resolution would have to occur through expanded state regulatory efforts independent of section 404, or would require negotiations with the Corps of Engineers to ensure greater deference to state concerns.

In Oregon, state agencies, the EPA, and USACE could not agree on the methodology to delineate the boundaries of wetlands. In addition to this basic methodological problem, other problems with assumption were identified. There were differing expectations of the state program, mission and philosophy that would create problems in the public and between state and federal regulating agencies. Some possible benefits from assumption also emerged from the state's scenario writing. Simplified, timely, consistent, decisions might be realized if the program were properly designed, and assumption did present an opportunity for stronger commitment by resource preservation interests coupled with the benefits derived by the regulated public from working with only one agency. In 1988 Oregon concluded that assumption did not resolve the coordination and implementation problems found under USACE permitting.

Kentucky

According to estimates of the State Division of Water, Kentucky lost approximately 58 percent of its 1.6 million acres of wetlands between 1790 and 1980. Described as "too dry to float and too wet to plow" by settlers, these wetlands, located primarily in the western part of the state were the victim of settlers clearing for farming and plantation tobacco cropping. Although most of the state's wetlands had been destroyed, Kentucky has taken steps to regulate its remaining wetlands. In 1975, the Commonwealth incorporated wetlands into the state surface water definition. By 1986, the state Division of Water entered into a Memorandum of Agreement with Kentucky Nature Preserve Commission devises wetland protection strategy. In 1988, the commonwealth choose not to assume the section 404 program, due to insufficient resources. The state continued to develop wetlands protection measures, such as Advanced Identification (ADID) in four western coal field counties. The state currently issues the section 401 water quality certificate, and believes it has sufficient authority to assume section 404.

The state has assumed all Clean Water Act responsibilities except for section 404 wetlands protection. In Kentucky, the Corps of Engineers averaged 131 permits per year from 1983 to 1988; 47 percent of permits were issued by the Louisville district office. The cost to the state for administering section 404, if assumed, was estimated to be approximately $406,000 (1988 dollars). The Division of Water was the logical assuming body, and no new legislation would be required to assume section 404. Although the state could actually expand its wetlands coverage by assuming section 404, funding and staff resources were primary impediments to the assumption of the 404 program.

In studying assumption, a primary concern of the state was whether section 404 assumption alone provided sufficient wetlands protection. The state's own feasibility study noted prominently that section 10 and section 404 permits are often processed concurrently by USACE because of overlapping coverage. Kentucky is covered by four USACE districts—Huntington, Louisville, Nashville, and Memphis. The U.S. Coast Guard has review and comment authority under section 404(3)(F), and TVA issues comment on permit applications under section 26 of the TVA Act (Durant, 1985). However, most concerns are handled through the Corps of Engineers via applicant communications instead of through formal hearings. The state report noted that

> Although part of EPA's role in the 404 program is to assist in making difficult interpretations of [section 404] (b)(1) provisions, applying them from one case to the next and establishing and maintaining consistency are most difficult. At the same time, consistency in applying the guidelines is crucial to the legitimacy and credibility of the 404 program as a whole.

For Kentucky, assumption of 404 might unify a highly fractured permitting process that involves up to five federal agencies and over a dozen different district, divisional, and regional offices of those agencies.

The authors of the Kentucky report (1988) identified a variety of deficiencies in the current section 404 program as administered by the Corps of Engineers. The USACE jurisdiction does not cover many slow moving streams that serve as breeding areas and habitats for a variety of fish species. State analysts also noted shortcomings in the provisions governing dredging. Under section 404, equipment that does not enter the stream channel and deposits material above the high-water line is not covered by section 404. The state viewed this loophole as opening the way for degradation of wetlands.

State regulators also noted that the regulated public often confuses the NPDES program with the section 404 program. Finally, Kentucky analysts noted a problem associated with assumption decisions in New Jersey, Michigan, and Maryland. Overuse of nationwide permits results in a "great deal of unknown activity in Kentucky's streams and wetlands." Assumption would have preempted the use of nationwide permits and eliminate this problem. Still, despite the potential resource and administrative benefits to be obtained from section 404 assumption, the cost of assumption precluded the state from further action.

Minnesota

In 1987 the Minnesota state legislature authorized the study of feasibility of section 404 assumption (Minnesota DNR, 1989). The state report indicated that two to three years would be required to prepare for assumption, including the development of new regulations and procedures. The state agency responsible for wetlands regulation recommended against assumption, and indicated three reasons for opposing assumption:

- Increased cost and the lack of federal funding;
- Over-intrusive state and federal reporting requirements;
- The controversial history of the program.

In addition, the state noted that the assumption of section 404 could create a dual permitting standard in the state.

Minnesota indicated four conditions that the federal government must be meet before the state would assume section 404. First, the federal government must provide 50 percent of the annual costs of section 404. Second, the federal government must relinquish veto power to the state and allow the state to make the final determination on any permit. Third, Federal government must provide an inventory map which preidentifies all section 404 waters, and indicates assumable and non-assumable waters. Finally, there should be a federal expansion of activities covered by section 404.

Assumption of the section 404 program by the state would expand the regulatory responsibility of the state from 3.5 million acres of wetlands to 8.7 million acres of wetlands. The state does not have not have sufficient statutory authority to assume section 404. For assumption to proceed, Minnesota will need to adopt legislation that:

- Gives the state sufficient authority to assume;

- Expands the scope and size of fines the state can issue;

- Creates ditch maintenance provisions for the permitting process.

Also, the state may want to extend its existing drainage provisions into assumable waters.

The significant benefits of section 404 assumption for Minnesota are the reduction of duplication and delays in the permitting system and the elimination of many "surprise" permit requirements. Other advantages include the streamlining of authority over wetlands; the state could expand the range of its new wetbank program into Phase II and Phase III waters; all fines that are presently levied for discharge and fill violations will go into the state general fund; the state will be able to impose stricter enforcement and access to wetlands resources; and, the section 401 permit and the entire agency that issues that permit (the Minnesota Pollution Control Agency) can be eliminated.

There are also several disadvantages to assuming the section 404 program. First and foremost is cost. State outlays for wetlands regulation under an assumed program were nearly prohibitive. The additional costs of section 404 assumption were estimated at between $860,000 and $1.3 million, plus outlays for two to three years of greater than $70,000 for application preparation. The EPA veto over permit decisions remains in place, as does extensive EPA oversight, and the potential for public opinion fallout due to confusion between federal and state procedures is heightened.

A particularly thorny legal issue noted in the Minnesota report is the impact of future revisions of the Clean Water Act on state-assumed programs. Future changes in the federal section 404 program will necessitate that the state change its regulations in order to stay in compliance with a Memorandum of Agreement. Were Minnesota to fail to revise non-compliant sections of its regulations, the state's program could be turned back over to the Corps of Engineers.

Alabama

Alabama uses a joint permit application program, operated with the Corps of Engineers (O'Toole, 1991). The state is covered by the Nashville and Mobile districts. Although the state has no wetlands regulation program, the Alabama Department of Environmental Management (ADEM) conducts section 401 review for the state, and can use the 401 permit to control which projects are considered for section 404 permits. The TVA is also involved in many permitting decisions in the northern part of the state (section 26a of the TVA Act). The Corps of Engineers handles all delineations, and most section 404 applications in Alabama also require a section 10 permit under the Rivers and Harbors Act (O'Toole, 1991).

According to the Alabama study, only a small minority of 404 public review permits would be eligible for transfer to the state. If the state assumed section 404 responsibility, an additional decision point would be created in the implementation process. Delays would ensue because some cases would have to wait for jurisdictional determination, a problem also noted by Kentucky officials (Kentucky DEP, 1988). For some assumable Phase I waters, the USACE would retain authority in waters regulated under section 10 of the Rivers and Harbors Act, resulting in a split permit. The TVA would still be involved in many northern Alabama cases. In these cases, permitting in northern Alabama becomes more confounded since the Corps of Engineers retains some jurisdiction, the state assumes some waters, and the TVA may overlap with either or both. In addition, all three entities could be involved in projects where the TVA has authority and the water is an assumable phase I body with section 10 jurisdiction allocated to the USACE.

In Alabama, the lack of programs related to section 404 makes assumption unattractive. Extensive programmatic changes and legislation are necessary for the state to assume section 404. Alabama has no independent wetlands program. Also, the Alabama Department of Environmental Management (ADEM) is perceived by the regulated community to be highly vulnerable to political influence.

Assumption for Alabama also will result in a variety of new expenditures, while few redundancies in state/federal procedures are eliminated. The cost of assumption ranges from $300,000–500,000 per annum, plus an additional $100,000–200,000 in startup costs. The state has no certain sources of additional funding.

Another problem identified by the Alabama study was the loss of federal endangered species protection in assumable waters, a concern in other states we studied. The EPA region 4 office indicated that a state assumption plan that did not include resource protection "at least" as stringent as provided under federal law would not be approved. Endangered species protection is an additional complication that Alabama would have to address prior to enacting state legislation supporting assumption. Conversations with a state regulator indicated that the state rejected assumption because of the "political vulnerability" of the state agency, a desire by the regulated public to see the current system retained, and because the state already possessed a "powerful tool to regulate federal permit activity" in wetlands through the section 401 water quality certificate.

Nebraska

Nebraska has a long history of wetlands protection activity. Wetlands protection dates back at least to the Bureau of Fish and Wildlife "Duckstamp" program. Nebraska wetland resources are also clearly identified and well-documented. The first inventory of the state's wetlands was made in 1955 by the Fish and Wildlife Service, and subsequent inventories were compiled in the 1960s, and 1970s. Nebraska also has been active in federal water policy initiatives, and by 1982 the state had assumed all Clean Water Act responsibility except for administration of section 404. No legislative barriers precluded the state from assumption of section 404. However, the primary threat to Nebraska wetlands (drainage) was not addressed by section 404 assumption.

The state permit load would increase slightly under section 404 assumption. Of the 197 Corps of Engineers section 404 permits were issued in Nebraska, 145 were for waters other than the Missouri River, which constitutes the only phase I waters in Nebraska. Annual costs to the state would increase by approximately $125,000, a savings of almost $6,000 in total public expenditures; unless otherwise noted, all financial data are in constant 1990 dollars. Total costs to the Corps of Engineers for the administration of its 404 program were $330,000 in 1979 and $275,000 in 1981. In 1982, costs of administering non-phase I waters was approximately $192,000. The estimated cost of assumption in Nebraska was $141,000.

Like Kentucky and Alabama, Nebraska administers the section 401 water quality certification program, which serves as an effective veto of any project that would be permitted under section 404. between 10 percent and 30 percent of section 401 permits are issues after-the-fact. As in most states, USACE seldom issues permits over the vigorous objections of state agencies, and delays the 404 decision until after state permits and 401 water quality certification are received.

In Nebraska, an estimated 48 staff hours go into processing each individual permit. USACE has sought to streamline process by applying nationwide and general permits and making use of preapplication conferences. If multiple draftings of applications and revisions are eliminated, the processing of an application can proceed substantially faster. The costs of the 404 program are closely tied to the rate of individual permit applications. Approximately 75 percent of the state costs in administering section 404 derived from assumable waters.

Although assumption could be obtained with little effort and at a recuced cost to the state, assumption did not go forward. Conversations with Nebraska regulators indicated that there were two reasons assumption did not procede. First, the greatest environmental threat confronting Nebraska wetlands is not dredge and fill, but drainage, which is not regulated by section 404. Even if the state assumed 404, they would not be able to confront this problem without additional legislation. The other reason that Nebraska bypassed assumption was that relations between the state water agencies and the Corps of Engineers improved dramatically in the early 1980s. Before 1982, the state often found itself in conflict with the Corps district office. According to a state official, relations with the USACE district improved subsequent to the study of assumption, in part because of the rotation of the district engineer at the USACE.

South Carolina

Approximately 23 percent of South Carolina is wetlands (4.7 million acres). The aggregate loss of wetlands in the state is not as significant as in many other states; consequently, the state study indicated that the threat of development is not as great in South Carolina. The state still has most of the wetlands it possessed 200 years ago. One Corps of Engineers district (Charleston) administers all of section 404 in South Carolina, except for the Savannah River Basin, which is non-assumable and administered by the Savannah, Georgia

USACE district. The eight coastal counties of South Carolina constitute a coastal zone management district, which shares joint permitting authority with USACE. An individual permit is required for any discharge in the eight-county coastal management zone, including discharges normally covered under general or nationwide permits. The South Carolina Department of Health and Environmental Control (SCDHEC) reviews all section 404 permit applications to issue section 401 water quality certification. This process includes a preapplication process, which facilitates preparing applicant success in obtaining favorable permit decisions. Mistakes or possible areas of conflict are identified in advance.

South Carolina has the legal authority to assume section 404 at the state level. The state already assumed the section 402 NPDES program before examining section 404 assumption. However, the limitation on assumption regarding tidal and navigable waters is a disincentive to assumption by the state. As with other states we have studied, the lack of federal funding and state budgetary and jurisdictional problems weighed against section 404 assumption. South Carolina opted not to proceed with taking over the dredge and fill program.

The South Carolina feasibility study noted similarities between the section 402 program and the section 404 program. South Carolina assumed NPDES authority in 1975, and grants a five-year permit. The evaluative and administrative procedures for NPDES are similar to section 404, and would ease state assumption, should it ever occur. The program submission requirements for 404 assumption are similar to those for section 402. State implementors believed that the section 402 assumption model and processes could expedite assumption. Assumption of section 404 eliminates the state 401 water quality certification program and streamlines the permit process. Section 404 assumption extends departmental involvement to isolated wetlands.

South Carolina regulators had several concerns about assumption that deterred the state from assuming the program. As with other states, the inability to attempt partial assumption was a significant barrier, as was the retention by the Corps of Engineers of its jurisdiction over all phase I waters (section 10 waters). Analysts for South Carolina determined that assumption was not necessary for the state to extend its authority under the existing state permitting system, especially if South Carolina did not expand the scope of wetlands regulation. Without assumption, the state can withhold certification of a wetlands project through the Section 401 water quality certificate. And, because over 90 percent of all section 404 activities in South Carolina require some form of state permit, the state continued to have input on a variety of wetlands regulatory decisions without taking over section 404.

North Carolina

North Carolina undertook a study of section 404 assumption in 1985. At the time assumption was considered, the state was already operating a joint permit application program with the Corps of Engineers, and twenty coastal counties of the state were in a Coastal Zone Management program. State law constrains the extent that section 404 assumption can serve as a basis for expanded wetlands protection. At the time of the study, an assumed 404 program in North Carolina was limited by state statute to the minimum scope allowed under federal law; no enhancement of resource protection is likely to occur in North Carolina's pro-business, pro-agriculture politics (see Luebke, 1990). The state law had more restrictive application of environmental impact analysis (EIS) including the exclusion of private projects from EIS requirements.

One of the main problems with North Carolina entering the assumption process is the fractured nature of the state's environmental protection bureaucracy. Twelve state agencies have to review and comment on section 404 permits. State assumption does little to streamline the process, and the state has large numbers of non-assumable phase I waters. Options for North Carolina to section 404 assumption include:

- The creation of a new agency, which would require enacting legislation;

- Having one agency assume 404 maintain coastal management arrangement between the USACE and the North Carolina Department of Coastal Management;

- Developing a coordination unit to direct permit applications to the proper state or federal agency.

In considering assumption of the federal program, the state financed a feasibility study on state assumption of 404. The results of this study indicated that, while assumption was technically possible, a variety of limitations to assumption existed that derived from the structure of state regulation and the inability to pass new legislation to meet federal assumption standards.

Wisconsin

In 1990, Wisconsin examined the possibility of assuming the 404 program from the federal government. Between 60 and 70 percent of the state's wetlands lie outside of the current jurisdiction of the state. A dramatic increase in state jurisdiction and wetland regulation activity would occur with 404 assumption by the state. Wisconsin requires an individual permit for all regulated activities; general permits are available for activities covered by federal nation-wide permits. The state exempts all agricultural practices from permits.

There are differences in the state and federal permit review processes. The Corps of Engineers first determines the water dependence of the activity, then it determines possible alternatives to the water-affected site. Finally, USACE considers mitigation of the affected site. The Corps of Engineers also considers a public interest review. By comparison, the Wisconsin permitting system uses the public interest review as the first criterion for considering site permitting. The state places a priority on developing longterm water use for the majority of the people in the state. Under state rules, mitigation is only allowed for transportation projects. The prioritization of concerns in the Wisconsin system indicates a far more rigorous permit approval process than exists in the USACE system.

Wisconsin currently uses the section 401 water quality certificate to waive or deny certification of projects that do not violate state law. Over 30 percent of section 401 requests are declined. In 1990, the state adopted wetland water quality standards at the urging of the EPA. The state also uses joint mechanisms to influence the federal permit process and streamline the regulatory burden on the community, including a joint permit application program with the Corps of Engineers. Negotiations are currently underway to develop a statewide general permit similar to the one in place in Maryland. The state agency and the USACE engage in reciprocal notice on public hearings and public notices.

Wisconsin is engaged in extensive cooperative activity with the Fish and Wildlife Service and EPA. The state concluded an MOA with the USFWS that expedites the implementation of the Fish and

Wildlife Coordination Act. The state forwards all section 401 decisions directly to the EPA, and EPA and state regulator comments on specific 404 applications are reciprocally exchanged. Most recently, the state and the EPA entered into cooperative development of the Green Bay wetland inventory and water quality standards. The state program does not have as broad of jurisdiction as the federal program, and therefore affects fewer waters.

Wisconsin water protection officials think streamlining can improve resource protection, but Wisconsin will need additional resources, especially staff, to handle the increased workload from a streamlined program. Local officials indicated that the identification, delineation, and education about permissible activities are the main problems with wetlands resource protection.

State regulators indicated that a high degree of confusion occurs in the existing bifurcated state/federal permit system. Applicants do not necessarily know what kind of permits they need when they apply for permits. Regulators readily acknowledge that streamlining the permit process can eliminate a great deal of frustration for the regulated public. Despite the enthusiasm for assumption among Wisconsin Department of Natural Resources (WDNR) officials, the limitations on state authority and the costs of assumption again emerge as powerful deterrents to assuming section 404.

The officials at the WDNR indicated that they are prepared to take over the federal program, and that such an assumption would benefit the public. As was reiterated in many of our interviews, state staff indicated that they thought they have a better understanding of the federal program than the federal officials do of the state program. They conceded that state standards are not as clear as federal standards. However, because federal standards are not applied in a rigorous or consistent fashion, the effectiveness of clear federal regulations is compromised. State officials feel that they can compliment federal statutory clarity with their own rigorous implementation habits. The state evaluation study noted problems with the USACE-implemented 404 program that confirmed the observations of other state and federal sources. Wisconsin evaluators observed that the Fish and Wildlife Service is diligent about monitoring and documenting violations of permits issued by the USACE. If the USFWS notes a violation, they contact the Corps of Engineers, and then send a map indicating the violation area and the date of the violation. By comparison, the USACE is not consistent in surveillance or notification of violations to other relevant agencies.

State assumption of the 404 program will increase the cost of resource protection for the state. Wisconsin will have to expand the number of field staff, and increase appropriations to implement an assumed program. In 1993, the Corps of Engineers budgeted $1.1 million and 15 staffers for enforcing section 404 in Wisconsin. The state Department of Natural Resources budgeted $3.8 million and 34 staff for all of its water projects, and 64 percent of state staff time was spent on wetland permitting.

Wisconsin regulators noted a variety of advantages and disadvantages to state assumption of 404, as well as necessary changes to the state permitting system necessary for assumption. State assumption would require changes in the state system that processes permits. State assumption would indicate a move away from nationwide and general permits and toward the use of all individual permits. State monitoring activity would increase dramatically. There would be a decrease in the replication of local permits as the state moved toward joint local-state permitting, and assumption would lessen the number of permit stops required of the regulated community; the number of agencies involved in many wetlands permit decisions would be reduced; and, the nationwide permits would be eliminated from the state permitting system, thereby insuring greater scrutiny of activities in the resource.

Assumption is not without disadvantages. Costs would increase dramatically under an assumed program, and the regulatory burden would overwhelm the existing state permitting structure. The state Department of Natural Resources could become subject to increased political pressure from local interests and state legislators, who exercise sway over the funding of the program. The Corps of Engineers would retain all section 10 waters, resulting in the continuation of a bifurcated permitting process (see also O'Toole, 1991). And, any changes in federal regulation would necessitate changes in state statutes governing wetlands. These last two points in particular would enhance the continued fracturization of the permitting process and difficulty in ascribing administrative accountability, even after assumption.

Among the state implementors, local agencies, and policy makers questioned, only the Wisconsin DNR staff supported assumption. Other commenting agents and actors indicated that stop-gap measures, such a joint permitting, would be a less expensive way to improve both state wetlands protection and increase efficiency in the permit process. The prospects of EPA oversight and the controversy surrounding the program contributed to the decision to recommend against assumption. According to Wisconsin water quality officials, when the controversy of the program was considered with the cost of assuming section 404, the state opted against assumption.

The state identified alternative policy actions to the assumption of section 404 that can improve resource protection and the permitting process. These activities would not increase state costs as much as assumption, but apparently would improve the efficiency and effectiveness of state resource protection efforts. These activities include joint tracking of permits by the state and the USACE; mapping and inventory of state wetlands resources; and the development of an interagency coordination mechanism to cut down on duplicative efforts by the USACE, USFWS, and state agencies involved in wetlands protection and regulation. This effort is not unlike what is currently underway in Florida.

Lessons from Other States

In the eight states we examined that considered and then rejected assumption, seven indicated that the state financial obligations to startup and maintain the program would increase. Although cost was not the only rationale for opposing assumption—Nebraska actually indicated that assumption would save money overall—the lack of federal funding to support and assist assumed programs underscored for the states the cost they would assume for increased staff and other obligations. As Table 6-1 reveals, of the 12 states we examined that considered assumption, only one estimated no net increase in costs due to assumption of the 404 program. Every state except Maryland indicated that an increase in personnel resources would be necessary to achieve successful assumption of wetlands permitting authority on a consolidated basis.

In addition to the lack of financial incentive for assuming the section 404 program, the states have few other positive reasons for pursuing assumption. These disincentives are related to a variety of factors, including: the authority that the state will exercise in administering the program; the "negative" image associated with the existing 404 program; the limits of section 404 assumption to enhance the protection of state wetlands; the potential for expanded, rather than reduced and streamlined bureaucratic burden on the regulated public; and, the inability to tailor assumption to fit the regulatory, environmental, and legal needs of the individual states. Given the lack of discretion provided states to craft regulations governing wetlands, it is not surprising that state governments would reject assuming more responsibility to implement regulations designed by the federal government. In fact, the real surprise is that Michigan and New Jersey opted to assume responsibility for the 404 program.

Table 6-1 The Costs of Section 404 Assumption

State	Year of assumption study	Estimated costs*	Additional staff requirements
Nebraska	1982	$141,835	3
Michigan	1984	$462,041	5
North Carolina	1984	$856,205	17
South Carolina	1986	$375,754	9
New Jersey	1987	N/A	N/A
Oregon	1988	$471,176	9
Kentucky	1989	$427,963	7
Minnesota	1989	$1,369,980	19
Alabama	1991	$512,344	10
Wisconsin	1993	$1,650,000	15–22
Maryland	1994	-0-	0
Florida	1994	$1,000,000–2,000,000	N/A

*1990 dollars

Incomplete Authority

State programs do not retain the same level or scope of authority as the Corps of Engineers when assuming section 404. For many states, authority problems arise from four primary factors:

- The issue of non-assumable waters;

- The five-year limit on the terms of a state-issued permit;

- The retention by the EPA of the final decision granting a permit;

- Problems with delineation.

Virtually every state considering assumption asserted, either in its own feasibility studies or during our field interviews, that the USACE had problems with the quality and consistency of its permitting process. Inconsistent permitting decisions, a failure to apply section 404 criteria to decisions, and a lack of enforcement against persistent and repeat violators fed the perception of inadequate implementation. For these states, the incentive to assume the 404 program directly relates to a desire to remove responsibility for the process from the USACE. This motivation disappeared or was substantially weakened when states learned the extent to which the Corps of Engineers would continue to be involved in the regulation of state wetlands in phase I waters. Strong incentive for states to assume the 404 program appears to be virtually nonexistent. For example, in the waters that the states can assume, the state will not be able to issue longterm permits—unlike USACE—or be able to exercise the same level of autonomy. By comparison, the Corps of Engineers can and often does override EPA objections on permitting decisions, despite the fact that EPA has oversight authority for the program. In Maryland, for instance, where the SPGP joint permitting program has been in place since 1991, conflicts continue to arise between USACE officials who want to issue nationwide permits to cover projects that state officials feel should be subject to the more stringent individual permits. As a result, the degree of actual discretionary authority granted to states opting to assume responsibility for the 404 program may be illusory.

The states also can expect to be subject to more intense oversight of section 404 programs than the Corps of Engineers. In Michigan and New Jersey, the EPA required adherence to a regulatory and oversight standard that was not enforced on the Corps of Engineers. The EPA still reviews every permitting decision of the state of New Jersey and Michigan, and other federal resource agencies have similar access.

The final authority problem is delineation. States must at least adhere to the delineation of wetlands used by the EPA. The USACE was not forced to adhere to the EPA/FWS delineation standard until 1990, when a scathing inspector general report (1990) made public the problems related to delineation enforcement under 404. States that move forward with section 404 assumption will often have a broader delineation and methodology that encompasses and ges beyond the EPA definition. Often these states will make use of buffer zones to minimize delineation error. Differences in methodology are sufficient to make assumption unattractive in states such as Florida, and these differences can lead to an unwillingness on the part of the state to change its delineation (see chapter 5).

Negative Program Image

The section 404 program has historically been beset by controversy (see chapter 2). Arbitrary Corps of Engineers enforcement, negative permit decisions, the failure to protect wetlands resources, and disregard for the objections of other agencies are often cited as the principal shortcomings of the USACE-implemented program. Section 404 is very controversial for its impact on the use of private property (takings) and its lack of responsiveness to local land-use programs. The level of controversy generated by the 404 program makes states loathe to assume responsibility without sufficient financial compensation or definitive regulatory authority over final decisions. As legislatures and agencies seek to contend with divisive and hostile constituencies, the likelihood of any state taking on the challenge of section 404 is remote.

The Limits of 404 Assumption

Assumption of the 404 program alone does little to protect wetlands. A state must also enact wetlands laws that expand the activities covered by permits or considers the cumulative effects of permitted activities. Otherwise, assumption will do little to enhance wetlands protection beyond the ability of the state to improve implementation in phase II and phase III waters. For example, substantial damage to wetlands occurs due to the cumulative effects of minor activities currently governed by nationwide permits. If assumption does not include the expansion of regulated activities, conversion activities that do not include dredge and fill will continue unabated. Extensive site inspection and monitoring of "minor" activities should enhance wetlands protection, as it has in Michigan. Still, these activities are beyond the purview of simple assumption of the 404 program.

Potential for Increased Bureaucratic Burden

In several of the states examined, the assumption of the 404 program would heighten the potential for increased bureaucratic confusion. This outcome was considered likely in coastal states such as Oregon, North Carolina, and South Carolina, where Corps would retain jurisdiction over substantial waters. In Alabama and Kentucky, where the jurisdiction of the state, USACE, and TVA would overlap in various configurations, confusion might also occur over what agency the regulated community should apply to and who has lead agency authority for specific permits.

Customizing Assumption

A principal criticism of the section 404 assumption process is that it is relatively inflexible. When a state assumes the 404 program, it is locked into full assumption of all non-Phase I waters in the state. Partial assumption is not an option. States are forced to grant only short-term permits compared to those of longer duration allowed under Corps of Engineers permitting authority. And, states may have to change the scope of their existing water programs to cover wetlands. Interviews in many states noted the loss of supporting federal procedures, expertise, and resources as another factor that makes the all-or-nothing approach to 404 assumption unattractive from a state perspective. The perceived lack of flexibility seemingly forces state regulators into either or choices that typically result in the continued prevalence of the status quo, in this case continued USACE administration of section 404.

"Assumption? Why Bother?"

The process of assumption takes on some of the characteristics of the communications model described in chapter 1: the states have avenues to seek alteration of the regulatory environment, and have the capacity to initiate change from the bottom. However, the problem with assumption emerges less from the ability to work with federal agencies, and more so with the range of possible options afforded the states are rather limited, being in fact only three: (1) *status quo* regulation through the federal, USACE-administered program; (2) obtaining a state programmatic general permit; or (3) assumption of federal authority in non-phase I waters. In all three instances the scope of regulation is constrained by federal standards, which preempt creative alternatives to wetland protection. Even when the authority for the program devolves to the states, it is the top-level agencies that are exercising final control through the application of federal baseline standards, oversight, and the presence of a sunsetting provision in all state-assumed programs.

The decisions of all of the states described in this chapter highlight these problems. Minnesota in particular was most pointed in their evaluation of the problem with the assumed 404 program. The Minnesota assumption study clearly argued the necessity of the Corps of Engineer and the EPA to relinquish real authority in the area of wetland protection to make state assumption occur. This condition is implicit in other states that might benefit from assumed programs, and who often have more institutional experience dealing with these resources than the EPA. As we indicated in chapter 5, the existing Florida state program has a history of regulating long-term development in a state that has extensive wetland resources. Assumption could be beneficial to developers who now confront several permitting stops when building near water (a common enough occurrence in Florida). However, the state gives up too much autonomy over long-term projects, and cannot respond to the needs of developers if short-term permitting disappears. The range of possible outcomes under assumption does not include the regulatory needs of Florida. Unless top-level federal agencies are willing to relax their standards and become more flexible in program design, assumption will not happen.

States that seek to enhance the protection of wetland resources beyond national standards have easier-to-pursue options than section 404 assumption. The states can look to other options, including the very attractive SPGP program, to streamline the permitting process for the public while obtaining veto power over projects that might obtain Corps approval. The use of an SPGP has allowed the state of Maryland to attain one of its policy goals—the elimination of destructive national permits—without taking over an entire program. And, state regulations are an effective way of addressing problems not covered by section 404, such as the drainage of wetlands.

National preeminence in the protection of wetland resources precludes the states from relaxing resource protection standards below levels mandates in federal law. For states or interests seeking relief from federal standards, assumption is not an option. Many of the states that explored assumption, including both of the Carolinas, Louisiana, and Florida, have strong development interests that have been frustrated by federal standards. The existing structure of federal water quality legislation, by relying on a definition of waters that is based on the commere clause, precludes a weakening of standards. Even if the EPA agreed to such a relaxation, the potential for litigation is great, barring new federal legislation to roll back or eliminate federal standards.

The lack of movement to modify implementation of wetland protection through section 404 is a product of the lack of real options afforded by assumption. Beyond streamlining the process, the goals and priorities of the states—eliminating federal agencies that are capricious or arbitrary from the process, or relaxing national standards for delineation or permissible activities—are not addressed by assumption. The program is not an attractive alternative precisely because it does so little beyond altering the procedures for delivering existing policy.

7

Wetlands Regulation and Implementation Problems

It is a maxim of our municipal law, and, I believe, of universal law, that he who permits the end, permits of course the means, without which the end cannot be effected.

Thomas Jefferson, 1808

The critics of the wetlands regulatory program have performed a service to the country by highlighting the need for meaningful reform in the administration of wetland regulatory programs.

White House Office on Environmental Policy, 1993

This study emerged from our desire to understand why state assumption of the principal component of federal wetlands regulation—the section 404 program—has encountered strong resistance from the states. Dissatisfaction with the implementation of section 404 by the Corps of Engineers was expressed in all of the states we examined. Environmental groups, regulated industries, and state regulators expressed dissatisfaction with Corps implementation practices and permitting decisions. Environmental groups viewed the Corps delineation methods as too narrow, and believed that the Corps of Engineers was not rigorously enforcing section 404 to preserve wetlands resources. Builders and other regulated entities, as well as state officials, find Corps permitting decisions are often arbitrary and inconsistent. Yet, by most accounts, state assumption of permitting has met with mixed reaction, and is usually viewed as an inferior policy option by the states.

In this concluding chapter, we use the perspectives on implementation introduced in chapter 1 to frame our concluding discussion of wetland regulation. We take each major perspective on implementation—top-down, bottom-up, and the communications model—and use those perspectives to assess three aspects of implementing wetland protection. First, we consider the performance of existing federal wetland regulation through section 404 as success or failure, based on the assumptions of the perspectives on implementation initially discussed in chapter 1. We then discuss whether section 404 assumption by the states can help to reconcile the perceived shortcomings in regulating wetlands, again using the major implementation theories to frame the discussion. Then, we examine the process of assumption through the various implementation lenses, with a particular emphasis on assessing section 404 assumption as an example of the problems that can be encountered when implementing an alteration of the implementation process. In conclusion, we discuss the implications of this analysis for the implementation of reformulated policy.

Implementation Perspectives on Section 404

First and foremost, we have to wonder why the states have looked at section 404 assumption as an option, and also why the EPA has encouraged 404 assumption for almost 20 years. This study has identified many problems, some real, others perceived, that are associated with the national wetlands protection program. Are the problems with the section 404 program a product of implementation, or are they more generally products of dissatisfaction with the concept of national regulation? To help facilitate this discussion, in Table 7-1 we cross-reference the "key variables" identified in each of the major perspectives on implementation with the presence or absence of those attributes in the federal Corps-implemented and state-assumed programs respectively.

A convincing argument can be made for top-down implementation failure of section 404. The program, as operated by the Corps of

Engineers, has a history of non-adherence to standards, inconsistent enforcement of the rules under section 404, and poor communication with other agencies involved in the regulation of wetlands and water resources. However, the design of the section 404 program, its rules, and its goals are not necessarily the problem. Instead, it goes to other factors, especially oversight and resources, to account for the failure of 404's implementation.

Section 404 authority was delegated to the Corps of Engineers by the EPA. As the statutory agency, the EPA retained a role as the agency responsible for the success or failure of the program, while giving to Corps the day-to-day responsibility for implementing the program. The failure of the Corps of Engineers to adhere to EPA standards can be seen as a top-down failure by the Corps, which is presented with conflicting missions when implementing both section 10 (navigation, a commercial and national security concern) and section 404 (water quality, a public health concern). The failure of this program from the top-down comes from three directions: (1) entrusting the EPA with the authority to implement this program, without sufficient resources to directly implement the program; (2) the policy mission conflict within the Corps of Engineers that is created by implementing section 404 on behalf of the EPA; and (3) the inability of the EPA to properly engage in oversight of the Corps-implemented program, either due to a lack of resources or a lack of desire.

The first failure, the inability to implement due to a lack of resources for direct implementation, is not necessarily within the purview of the EPA. Agencies make budget requests, but the ability to obtain funding for new programs, especially large regulatory programs, is out of their control and in the hands of legislators. Further, the original scope of section 404 was limited by legislation and interpretation by federal agencies. It was the courts that dramatically expanded the scope of section 404 to encompass wetland protection, not the EPA or Congress (chapter 3).

The mission conflict confronted by the Corps of Engineers is both a top-down implementation failure and an example of the kind of failings noted by bottom-up–oriented researchers. This failure is a product of implementation design. The delegation to the Corps of Engineers of EPA's permitting authority made bureaucratic sense. The delivery of a new program is performed by going through an existing program that affected the target, thereby creating some streamlining within the federal bureaucracy. The consequential problem of mission conflict created the failure. As we have noted repeatedly in this study, the Corps of Engineers has a fundamentally different mission with regard to water resources, emphasizing resource management rather

Table 7-1: Indicators of Implementation Success in Wetland Protection and Assumption

Perspective/Variables:	EPA/Corps Implementation of Section 404	State-Assumed Section 404 Implementation	The Assumption Process
TOP-DOWN			
Clear program objectives	No. Legislation protects *water quality*, by regulating discharge and fill into waters; court interpretation expanded regulatory scope to encompass wetlands; there is no formal wetland protection law in the United States.	Yes: Turns over to the states permitting authority for section 404 in all non-phase-I wetlands. No: Same clarity problems as in EPA/Corps program. States can address this problem in designing their state-assumed program legislation.	Transfer to the states all regulatory authority over non-phase-I waters
Causal theory as basis of policy.	Yes. Causal theory of regulation is based on "best science"; courts, not legislature or agency, established policy rationale.	Yes; this is implicit in the need to have a program at least as rigorous as the federal government.	Yes. Streamlining process expedites process for the regulated public, reduces government.
Structures to Enhance Compliance	Formal review and oversight process between EPA and	EPA exercises more authority over state programs than over	Yes. EPA has final authority to approve an assumed

	Corps of Engineers; comment of other agencies; often this mechanism fails because principal agency has insufficient levers to compel compliance.	the Corps-implemented program. Most formal review and oversight mechanisms remain from federal program in place. Tougher oversight conducted with new programs.	program, subject to the advice and comment of USFWS, USACE, and other involved agencies. State cannot assume without EPA approval.
Commitment of Enforcement Officials	Strong commitment at EPA national office, and in some regions; Corps of Engineers, which conducts day-to-day implementation, has different and conflicting policy goals and agency mission.	High. State has to take initiative to assume federal program, so many of the preconditions of successful implementation are met before assumption. State programs always as tough or tougher than federal regulations.	Mixed. EPA has promoted assumption for two decades, but only two states have proceeded. Federal government is unwilling to alter federal standards to facilitate assumption.
Interest Group, Sovereign, agencies havePolitical Support	Most major environmental groups advocate a new national wetland regulation structure; regulated public is dissatisfied with current system; political leadership in Congress has attempted to alter program.	Variable by state and time. Strong in Michigan, questionable in New Jersey	Mixed. Federal agencies have been in conflict during assumption, likewise with interest groups. Strong political backing needed in states to pursue assumption.

(continued)

Table 7-1 (*Continued*)

Perspective/Variables:	EPA/Corps Implementation of Section 404	State-Assumed Section 404 Implementation	The Assumption Proces
TOP-DOWN			
Socio-Economic Changes that Undermine Political Support or Causal Theory	Scope of wetland regulation has affected many property owners, developers who advocate changing the law; majority in Congress is unfriendly to command-and-control environmental regulation; delineation and relative value problems (which wetlands should be protected?)	Loss of political support, funding, can result in EPA takeover of program; questions of delineation and relative value problems (which wetlands should be protected?)	N/A
BOTTOM-UP			
Field-Level Autonomy and Empowerment	Mixed. Program is structured with strict guidelines and delineations of resource to constrain bottom-level flexibility; in practice, the Corps of Engineers has shown	State programs, once established, have substantial latitude in implementation, as long as they maintain resource protection at levels *at least as high* as federal regulations.	Yes. At the federal level, much of the assumption MOA is worked out among state implementors, regional EPA and USFWS personnel, and district Corps personnel,

	great flexibility in applying standards of the program.			within constraints of federal regulations.
Broad Range of Policy Options	No.	States may implement any law or program that is tougher than the federal standards, but which does not violate federal law. EPA retains oversight and veto over changes in assumed programs.		Limited. Assumption of the federal program and the SPGP are the only real options. No partial assumption or modified standards are possible.
Generous Resources	Corps of Engineers has principal implementing authority of section 404 because (a) the Corps always regulated many of these resources under section 10 of the Rivers and Harbors Act, and (b) EPA lacked the resources and manpower to implement the program. Resources exist, but they do not enhance bottom-up ability to craft better policy.	Variable, but states are able to place more personnel into the field than the Corps of Engineers. Also, Corps personnel are freed from dealing with permits in non-phase-I waters. Most joint-project grants disappear under a funded program.		No. The federal government does not offer project grants of supplemental funding for assumed programs.

(continued)

Table 7-1 (*Continued*)

Perspective/Variables:	EPA/Corps Implementation of Section 404	State-Assumed Section 404 Implementation	The Assumption Proces
COMMUNICATIONS			
Avenues for Policy Feedback from Bottom to Top	Interaction of state and federal agencies in conducting permit decisions; formal oversight mechanism of EPA; Litigation.	Interaction of state and federal agencies in conducting permit decisions; formal oversight mechanism of EPA; Litigation	Iterative, proactive process that allows for feedback on assumption applications. The advice and comment of other federal agencies can result in an adversarial experience that emphasizes differences in agency mission and brings our institutionalized conflict.
Reformulation Processes	State assumption of authority; Statewide programmatic general permit.	Five-year sun-setting on state programs subjects it to periodic review and renegotiation of MOA.	N/A

| Democratic Legitimacy | Unclear; EPA is the agency with formal authority, and it has been held accountable for the conduct of the 404 program; Corps is often cited as the implementation problem, but EPA does not address Corps implementation failures. | Streamlined program brings fewer agencies into process, which makes program user friendly; bifurcated process under assumption means that federal agencies will be directly involved in some decisions, but not others. Devolution of program to states is symbolic of New Federalism. | N/A |

than resource protection. Day-to-day administration of section 404 creates competition between the primary mission of the Corps under Section 10 and the new secondary mission that came with section 404. The decision to implement section 404 through the Corps is a classic case of the kind of problem with implementation design that critics like Hjern (1982) have focused on for years. By forward mapping—starting with a policy at the top of a system and then navigating down through the existing agencies to reach the target—the goals of the original program are often displaced. The new policy has to be implemented by existing bureaucracies, which, as was the case of section 404, had very different policy missions. A better solution, advocates of bottom-up implementation argue, is to start from the target and design a system from the target up.

The failure of the EPA to engage in oversight is the more disturbing aspect of the top-down failures of section 404. The EPA evolved in the 1970s from a centralized regulatory agency, to instead become a "coordinating agency" for the implementation of environmental programs through other agencies. In effect, the EPA went into the business of conducting political oversight. If we look at their performance with the implementation of wetland protection, we see a failure of EPA to conduct its primary omission of implementing compliance and oversight. Both the General Accounting Office and the EPA's own inspector general noted that EPA had abdicated authority, especially in region 4.

By establishing itself as the principal *coordinating* agency for conducting federal environmental policy, the EPA necessarily sets itself up as a magnet for programmatic failures, whether those failures are due to policy design or policy implementation. In the case of section 404 regulation, there are numerous federal agencies involved in the comment on permits, and these agencies have competing missions and goals. When an agency is implementing policy on behalf of the EPA, it is reasonable to expect that the agency should seek the goals and enforce the standards established for the program by the EPA. When this does not happen—as was the case with Corps implementation of section 404—the EPA needs to be able to somehow coax or leverage the implementing agency into implementing the program as designed. With regard to the Corps of Engineers, EPA has limited leverage and therefore cannot compel the Corps to comply. So how does EPA attain better compliance in the implementation of its programmatic goals, given these constraints?

In the field of wetland protection, state assumption of the federal discharge and fill program is certainly one attractive option. By transferring the authority to implement section 404 to the states, the EPA is able to do what so many advocates of state assumption want: remove the Corps of Engineers from the regulation of large number of wetlands. This is a desirable outcome for EPA, because section 404 authority is located in agencies that have to demonstrate greater deference to the EPA; the agency can build an effective, top-down compliant implementation structure from the bottom up. The process of assuming section 404 assures that a more rigorous, effective wetland regulation program goes into place; to echo the complaint of New Jersey officials, EPA does hold the states to an ideal that is higher that the reality of Corps implementation in the application process, and in the initial (and continued) implementation of their program. A state seeking assumption has to satisfy the EPA. A state who fails in their implementation of an assumed program will confront severe oversight from the EPA, including the possible revoking of the state-assumed program.

The preeminence of the federal agency over the state agency, due to constitutional structure, makes it easier for the EPA to ensure that a program is implemented that will be in compliance with EPA standards and which will be sufficiently well-funded and politically-protected to effectively do the job of wetland protection. State assumption will not lead to a tremendous amount of autonomy for the states in crafting regulatory options, but the assumption option does represent an opportunity for bottom-up reformulation. The EPA, when acting with other agencies to craft an assumed program, is able to rectify many of the implementation problems associated with Corps implementation and ensure greater implementation success from a top-down perspective. In sum, from the perspective of EPA, section 404 assumption makes it possible to exercise policy levers to design a program that has a greater prospect for top-down implementation success.

From the states' perspective, implementation of section 404 does not work. The Corps of Engineers is inconsistent in the protection of resources, and the various agencies involved in wetland protection are as much in competition as in coordination. What is most troubling for states and regulatory targets, however, is the extent of federal regulation and application of federal standards without consideration of the particulars of the local environment, and the perceived failure of the EPA and Corps to recognize the expertise and skills of state agencies.

One of the most common complaints of states, when examining section 404 assumption, was that the EPA was inflexible on a variety of issues related to wetlands within their state. One of the best examples is delineation, the determining of what constitutes a wetland. In Maryland and Florida there is disagreement with the EPA regarding delineation of wetlands. In these states the EPA and Corps of Engineers regulate lands that the states do not consider to be wetlands. Whether in an existing federal wetland program, an SPGP, or a full assumption, a state cannot relax standards for environmental protection below those of federal law. We noted earlier in this discussion that bottom-up scholars argue that, in the crafting of an implementation, it is best to start with the target of policy, and then design a system to deliver policy to the target. The perception of bottom-up scholars is that field implementors and localized agencies have a better understanding of the policy problem to be addressed, and that those individuals require flexibility in designing programs to deliver policy. The national standards and top-down implementation of section 404 do not leave states with much room to modify existing policy. This makes the application of a bottom-up implementation strategy, which emphasizes variety and creativity in addressing problems at the local level, effectively impossible within the existing regulatory regime.

The one certainty about federal wetland protection is that many people are unhappy with the program. States find the implementation of the program by the Corps of Engineers districts to be often arbitrary. Among federal agencies there was a great deal of buck-passing by the principal agencies for implementation failures, and there is often disagreement between the EPA, the Corps of Engineer, USFWS, and the states regarding standards and goals of the programs. The states often feel that they are not empowered, and the perceptions of both the states and the regulated public is that the program as administered by the Corps of Engineers is implemented in a manner that is at best disorganized, at worst capricious and arbitrary.

Perspectives on State Goals: The Federalism Problem

There are a variety of problems in wetlands regulation that cannot be solved by state assumption of the federal 404 program. For example, section 404 assumption does not free the assuming state from federal environmental regulations or from the influence of the EPA and the Corps of Engineers. When a state assumes section 404 authority, the wetlands regulatory standards of the state must be at least as stringent as those authorized by EPA. The experiences of New Jersey, Maryland, and Michigan in pursuing assumption of the 404 program demonstrates that EPA regulators—who must approve the state program—hold states to a higher level of regulatory com-

petence than that exhibited by the Corps of Engineers. The existence
of a dual standard is evident in both the structure of the state-
assumed versus federal-operated system, and also in the perceptions
of state water officials. Or, as one senior state official asserted the
EPA has an "existing standard for Corps regulation and an ideal
standard for the states."

The most prominent example of a dual standard is the difference
in the time-limits on permits issued by the states in an assumes program, when compared to the much longer Corps of Engineers-issued
permits. The section 404 program operated by the federal government authorizes permitted activities for periods as long as 20 years.
A state-assumed program has a five-year limit on permitted activity.
It is reasonable to argue that the existence of a federal program that
operates through state agencies should have mechanisms for federal
oversight and control. The use of time-limited permits increases opportunities for oversight and review of state decisions. However,
EPA enforced no such standard in its delegation of day-to-day operational authority to the Corps of Engineers, which creates the perception of a paternalistic, rather than cooperative, arrangement
with regard to how the EPA treats the states.

It is the existence of states having different standards than the
Corps of Engineers that, ironically enough, compelled many states to
investigate assumption. Because the Corps has been inconsistent in
the application of EPA standards, several of the states examined in
chapters 5 and 6 looked to assumption as a vehicle to remove that
agency from the task of wetland protection. Unfortunately for those
states, assumption does not remove the Corps from regulating wetlands in most states. After assumption of section 404 by the state, the
Corps of Engineers retains jurisdiction over all phase I waters, which
it also regulates under Section 10 of the Rivers and Harbors Act (see
chapter 2). In fact, in some states with extensive wetlands, up to 70
percent of wetlands and waters are non-assumable and would remain
under Corps jurisdiction. And, EPA retains veto power over all permit
decisions in the states, as well as continued existence of the program.
The benefit for resource protection comes from the more stringent
application of standards and oversight to state-assumed programs.
From the perspective of the states, the incentives for assumption appear to be extremely limited, especially since the states would then
become the focal point for controversy surrounding decisions based
on regulations designed by federal agencies.

On balance, our analysis indicates that the limits on autonomy
imposed with state assumption of the section 404 discharge and fill
program is unlikely to give states sufficient incentive to pursue

assumption. Past experience indicates that the constraints placed on state regulators limit opportunities to modify federal policy, unless that modification further restricts activities within wetlands. In addition, few tangible inducements exist to promote state assumption without autonomy. State authorities, for example, are prevented from modifying discharge-and-fill regulation to address what are perceived to be existing implementation problems. States considering assumption also frequently lack the flexibility to generate the necessary funds to protect wetlands resources.Moreover, the property-rights and wise-use movements, especially in the west and south, limit the attractiveness to states of assuming and financing what is often perceived by its politically-active critics to be an onerous regulatory program.

The dynamics of state assumption should change dramatically if the federal government were to modify one or more of the statutes that govern the discharge-and-fill programs. For example, if the provisions of the Endangered Species Act were not applied to wetlands protection, the Fish and Wildlife Service would effectively be removed from the permit review process. The primary basis of wetlands protection under discharge and fill would return to the application of the hydrological model, which determines whether a discharge or fill would affect water quality (see chapter 2). Alternatively, were the states to have section 404 delegated to them by the EPA, it resultant implementation presumably would be affected by the unfunded mandates legislation enacted by the 104th Congress, although this legislation is largely symbolic.

The final resolution of state concerns with wetland regulation and state assumption will not likely be soon resolved. The set of conditions that many states seek to warrant pursuing assumption reside outside the range of possible policy options. They are not constitutionally-permissible, due to the use of the Commerce Clause as a rational for protecting the resource. By using constitutional preeminence as the basis for regulating wetlands, standards of federal law effectively constrain state law. Underlying the states demands for flexibility in the design of assumed wetland programs is a more general cry for less national government control in the federal system. The eradication of this barrier is beyond the purview of the state assumption process.

State Assumption: Preconditions and Lessons

When a state pursues assumption of the section 404 program, it should be able to meet several preconditions in order to expedite assumption. The assuming state agency should have clear statutory

authority to assume the program. The state permitting programs—
section 401, NPDES, and any other state permits—should be consolidated into a streamlined process. Unified political support for
assumption is essential, especially from the governor's office. And,
state regulatory officials should have a great deal of patience with
what has initially proven to be a very time-consuming process.

*The assuming state agency should have clear statutory authority
to assume 404.* In Michigan, New Jersey, and Maryland, legislation
and enacting statutes clearly defined assumption as a goal. In other
states that considered assumption such as Florida and North Carolina, the lack of clear statutory authority assigned to one lead
agency was a significant deterrent to assumption. However, legislative authority to assume section 404 may not be sufficient to guarantee assumption. As we observed in chapter four, Maryland had
sufficient capacity and legal authority to operate a 404 program.
However, the political barriers erected in the state senate derailed
assumption in the short term.

The failure of Maryland to formally request assumption legislation is not universally viewed as a failure, especially among environmental groups. In an article in the *National Wetlands Newsletter,*
Thomas Grasso and Grady McCallie (1994) of the Chesapeake Bay
Foundation hailed the legislature for stopping the passage of Maryland's assumption legislation. They asserted that a variety of flaws
in the regulations and in the state Department of Natural Resources' assessment of the costs of section 404 assumption would undermine the protection of wetland resources in the state. As we
noted in chapters 4 and 5, Maryland estimated no cost increase to
the state from assumption. Critics indicated that the state plan did
not include sufficient personnel resources to adequately protect the
resource. Like the New Jersey case, intense concerns were raised
about the potential exclusion of citizen participation and Fish and
Wildlife Service participation in the assumed program. Unless
Maryland can satisfy these critics or sway them to accept the state's
plan, political opposition by environmental groups remains likely.
Moreover, if the state passes enabling legislation that does not
clearly address the discrepancies in state and federal regulations
identified by environmental preservation critics, the potential for litigation or EPA rejection of the application is heightened.

*Streamlined state permitting mechanisms should contribute to a
successful state assumption.* In South Carolina and North Carolina,
the states were uncertain which of several agencies would take the
lead in an assumption. In Florida, the partitioning of water responsibilities between the Department of Environmental Regulation and

the Water Management Districts meant that state assumption of the federal program would not have eliminated the split-permitting program. Streamlining state regulatory procedures before pursuing assumption reduces confusion regarding delegation of intrastate activities. It also creates fewer potential decision nodes in the implementation process, and, reduces confusion for the regulated public.

The benefits of streamlining are also important from a theoretic standpoint. A recurring theme in the implementation literature, since the initial studies of the 1970s, has been the importance of communication within the network of implementing agencies. Pressman and Wildavsky (1973) argued that the reduction in the number of actors involved between the inception of policy and the delivery of services would benefit implementation. Their argument addressed hierarchies more than coordination between coequal agencies. However, when considered against the bottom-up perspective (delivering a service to the target), having a streamlined regulating agency will make it easier for the targets of regulation—those who engage in activities that affect wetlands—to identify their regulating agency. It will also ensure that coordination problems that arise from interagency rivalry and dispute are lessened, if not hopefully eliminated at the state government level.

A strong, favorable political consensus makes assumption more likely. As we observed in the New Jersey case, powerful political interests nearly undermined assumption by exerting political pressure on an incumbent governor seeking reelection. Similarly, if a state must pass additional legislation to clear the way for assumption, the potential for blockage of the program is heightened. Successfully moving an assumption proposal through the legislative process involves building a legislative coalition that clearly communicates the advantages derived from assumption, justifies the cost, and assures developers and preservation groups that their conflicting concerns will be addressed under assumption.

Even after legislation authorizing assumption by the state, there are still political hurdles to be surmounted in the process. As the New Jersey case demonstrated, the interagency politics among the Corps, the EPA, and the U.S. Fish and Wildlife Service can come into play. These agencies historically have divergent views of how to best protect wetlands resources.

Of all the political hurdles, the intergovernmental conflict between bureaucratic agencies will be the most difficult to overcome. This difficulty is a product of the relatively static nature of agency politics below the cabinet level. Throughout our discussion, we have returned to the role of agency mission and agency culture in affecting implementation of wetland both protection under 404 and assumption of 404 authority by the states. Compared to other political actors such as legislators, governors, and political appointees, many of the actors involved in the designing of assumption are career professionals who are relatively immune from political influence. The political differences held by the agencies involved in wetland protection are institutionalized, and less likely to be affected by external politics, unless tremendous political weight is brought to bear against agencies that are resistant to change.

Any state seeking assumption of the 404 program must be patient. From inception to completion, New Jersey assumption took over six years. Michigan assumption was a five-year process. Among likely candidates for the future, Maryland has been considering assumption for several years and is currently operating under an state programmatic general permit. Florida also is taking very deliberate steps toward assumption, but will not rush into the process. The measured, careful steps taken by these states are, in part, a reaction to the problems encountered by New Jersey when state officials rushed into assuming the Federal program. Our interviews with Florida and Maryland officials indicated that the states are reluctant to enter the political morass that made the New Jersey assumption such a tortured process.

Even without the extreme political resistance encountered by New Jersey, the assumption process is time consuming. Several federal agencies have the opportunity to comment on the state assumption plan. If the state plan in any way falls short of the specific requirements dictated by Clean Water Act regulations, then the state application will be rejected. During both the New Jersey and Michigan assumptions, applications were initially returned to the states to correct "minor" differences between federal and state regulations. The New Jersey application was further delayed by changes in the assumption rules that occurred during the application process.

An Implementation Perspective on the Assumption Process

The problems of section 404 implementation stem from the communication problems noted above. Clarity of communication between federal designers and local implementors is not assured. Moreover, the involvement of multiple federal and state perspectives does not promote consistency of interpretation or enforcement. The statute creates broad conditions for interpretation, and the definition of wetlands and their value varies among states and federal agencies. The procedures established according to federal statute are not always used, and the federal regulatory regime has been slow to modify itself in response to the complaints of state regulators.

The primary concern articulated by the regulated community and the states, consistency of implementation, is not met by the reform options offered by the EPA. As Goggin *et al.* (1990) note, four conditions need to be met for policy redesign to occur:

- An existing policy

- Some degree of dissatisfaction with the policy

- Communications from agents in the states—elected and appointed officials, often acting as intermediaries for organized interests, including clients and atetntive publics who would be affected by either maintaining or changing the status quo—to principals in Washington

- action in Congress and/or an executive branch agency in response to pressure from constituents in the states

In the case of section 404, the first three conditions have been in place for some time. For at least fifteen years, the states have made suggestions to the EPA about changes that might provide incentives for states to assume to promote the assumption of section 404 authority. These suggestions normally involve allocating federal funds to assist in the development of a state consolidated permitting program, relaxing the rules of assumption to allow the states to assume full permitting authority in waters regualted by the USACE, and allowing the state greater latitude in developing wetlands delineation standards. Each of these suggestions reflects an assumption widely shared by state officials that permeates this study: state officials believe that they are better positioned to effectively and consistently enforce the protection of wetlands, and feel that inconsistency in implementation by federal agencies is the greatest barrier to effective implementation.

If federal agencies are involved in the process of delegating programmatic authority and responsibilities to the state, the potential for substantial conflict exists among the federal agencies and between the states and the agencies. The U.S. Fish and Wildlife Service protest of New Jersey's assumption is an excellent example of the conflicts that can occur when a state seeks to obtain federal implementation authority. In this case, the Fish and Wildlife Service took the position that the New Jersey program was inadequate for purposes of wetlands protection, especially in the area of wildlife habitat. The service used a variety of political weapons at its disposal to block the state assumption effort which fostered a great deal of animosity between the service and state resource agencies.

The reaction of the USFWS demonstrates all of the characteristics of an agency responding to a perceived threat to its administrative turf. State officials in New Jersey and Maryland similarly characterized the behavior of the Corps of Engineers in their states. If states assume a larger role in the implementation and administration of programs that were previously the responsibility of federal agencies, those agencies are likely to attempt to protect their budgets and their agency missions. As a result, if states move to take greater responsibility for the section 404 program, they can expect resistance from federal agencies that perceive a real threat to their agency mission and their budgets unless the Congress actively circumscribes the federal role.

This lesson should not be lost on proponents of state assumption of established federal programs. At least in the case of wetlands protection, the option of turning regulation over to the states has meant a series of state-level skirmishes with Corps districts or Fish and Wildlife Service offices over procedural implementation and degree of resource protection afforded wetlands.

What bearing does this have on attempts to transfer the formulation, implementation, and administration of programs to the states? Our study demonstrates that, from the perspective of the states, the assumption process needs to be designed to minimize the ability of existing agencies to intervene to limit state discretion. Otherwise, states are not likely to willingly become responsible for being the focal point in decision making using regulations designed by federal agencies. Second, the states want to have sufficient latitude and autonomy to run programs within the same bureaucratic constraints as the federal agencies. States implementors are not interested in become adjuncts to federal agencies. They are demanding latitude in the formulation of specific policy design, and autonomy from extensive intervention by federal agencies. Many of the states examined in chapters 5 and 6 termed these to be preconditions for assumption. They are, in fact, more than preconditions. These terms, laid out most plainly in the Minnesota case but reiterated elsewhere, constitute an expression of a change in federal philosophy. The states will not willingly take on more regulatory burdens from the government without compensation and autonomy.

So how do we improve policy for wetland protection? Concerns about wetland policy that drive the examination of assumption are typically related to: (1) the scope of existing regulation under a federally-operated program; and (2) the consistency and effectiveness of implementation by federal agencies. Of these two problems, only one can be addressed through improvements in implementation. And, it does not matter which problem or which implementation paradigm that is chosen; only one can be solved.

Existing wetland policy is established indirectly through federal law, as interpreted by the federal courts in their expansion of the scope of the Clean Water Act to reflect the best available scientific knowledge about water resources. It is possible for the states to regulate activities in waters and wetlands beyond the scope of federal policy; it is not permissible to reduce the scope of federal regulation. Several of the states examined in this study have wetland laws that extend beyond federal law, and many of the states that examined wetland protection did so with at least an implicit intention to try and limit the scope of wetland protection, rather than to expand it. If the desire of states is to expand environmental protection, then the crafting of bottom-up solutions to address wetland protection is entirely possible. State policy which enhances federal authority is constitutional, and indeed such policy can benefit from the state assumption program. The other problem, the consistency of federal implementation, cannot be addressed by a bottom-up solution. The major problem with section 404, according to EPA and GAO auditors, was inconsistency in the application of standards. To address this problem necessitates crafting a program that the top of the administrative hierarchy can control and oversee, in order to enforce national standards. The potential for variability of standards under a bottom-up implementation only enhances the problems currently observed in wetland protection, namely the lack of consistent standards and enforcement.

These two approaches to improving implementation are not mutually exclusive, but they represent constraints on fixing public policy. The state assumption of wetland regulation under 404 allows the EPA to design new regulation from the bottom up. Such an approach actually helps the EPA improve top-down compliance. Similarly, the EPA needs the initiative of the states to proceed with policy redesign from the bottom-up. The EPA cannot act unilaterally to shift the regulatory burden. This is the final irony of implementation: bottom-up solutions, which often result in workable procedures to address problems, cannot be pursued with only top-down initiative; top-down solutions constrain the range of viable options to fix implementation from the bottom.

References

Anderson, William B. (1973). *The Wildman from Sugar Creek*. Baton Rouge: Louisiana State University Press.

Bostwick, Peg. (1989). Michigan's Section 404 Program Update. *National Wetlands Newsletter* 11(July–August): 5–7.

Brown, Stephen. (1989). Michigan: An Experiment in Section 404 Assumption. *National Wetlands Newsletter* 11 (July–August): 5–9.

Bullock, Charles S., III, and Charles Lamb, (eds.) 1985. *Implementing Civil Rights Policy*. New York: Brooks/Cole.

Cansler, Tim. (1997). *NLAP Alert: National Legislative Action Plan*. Louisville: Kentucky Farm Bureau.

Carson, Rachel. (1962). *Silent Spring*. Greenwich, CT: Fawcett.

Center for Environmental Studies. (1985). *404 Feasibility Study: Summary of the Final Project Report*. Raleigh: North Carolina State University.

Clean Water Amendments of 1995; Comprehensive Wetlands Conservation and Management Act of 1995 (H.R. 961).

Crampton, Lewis. (1984). Helping the States Carry a Bigger Load. *EPA Journal* 10 (January–February): 4–5.

Dahl, T. E., and C. E. Johnson. (1991). *Status and Trends of Wetlands in the United States, Mid-1970s to Mid-1980s*. U.S. Fish and Wildlife Service, Washington, D.C..

Dahl, T. E. (1991). *Wetland Resources of the United States*. St. Petersburg, FL: The Service.

Dean, Ray, and Lynn D. Frank. (1988). *State Assumption of the Federal 404 Permit Process*. Salem: Oregon Division of Lands (December).

Dye, Thomas R. (1990). *American Federalism: Competition Among Governments*. Lexington, MA: Lexington Books.

146 *References*

Elliott, E. Donald *et al.* (1985). Toward a Theory of Statutory Evolution: The Federalization of Environmental Law. *Journal of Law, Economics, and Organization* 1: 313.

Esty, Daniel C. (1996). Revitalizing Environmental Federalism. *Michigan Law Review* 95: 570–653.

Fitzgerald, Michael R., Amy Snyder McCabe, and David L. Folz. (1988). Federalism and the Environment: The View from the States. *State and Local Government Review* 20: 98–104.

The Florida House of Representatives Committee on Natural Resources. (1994). *Bill Analysis and Economic Impact Statement of HB 2875*. Tallahassee: The Florida House of Representatives (March 30).

———. (1994). *Final Bill Analysis and Economic Impact Statement of CS/CS/SB 1346*. Tallahassee: The Florida House of Representatives (April 25).

The Florida Senate Committee on Natural Resources and Conservation. (1991). *A Report on Wetlands Regulations in Florida*. Tallahassee: The Florida Senate (October).

———. (1990). *Review of Wetlands Permitting Activities of the Department of Environmental Regulation and the Water Management Districts*. Tallahassee: The Florida Senate (February).

Freshwater Wetlands Protection Act of 1987. (1987). Trenton: N.J.S.A. 13:9B-1 *et seq.*

General Accounting Office. (1988). *Wetlands: The Corps of Engineers Administration of the Section 404 Program* (GAO-RCED-88-110). Washington, D.C.: U.S. Congress, General Accounting Office.

Goggin, Malcolm L., Ann O'M. Bowman, James P. Lester, and Laurence J. O'Toole. (1990) *Implementation Theory and Practice: Toward A Third Generation.* Glenview, Ill.: Scott, Foresman.

Grasso, Thomas V., and Grady S. McCallie. (1994). Make No Assumptions. *National Wetlands Newsletter* 16 (May–June): 3–5.

Harrington, Hal. (1984). Michigan's 404 Program Assumption. *In Wetland Protection: Strengthening the Role of the States.* Gainesville, FL: Center for Governmental Responsibility, 488–92.

Harrington, Hal, and Betty J. Kennedy. (1988). Innovations in Michigan's Permitting. Paper presented at the U.S. EPA Wetlands Protection Program National Meeting (March/April).

Hays, Samuel. (1989). *Beauty, Health, and Permanence : Environmental Politics in the United States, 1955–1985.* New York: Cambridge University Press.

Hjern, Benny. (1982). Implementation Research—The Link Gone Missing. *Journal of Public Policy* 2:301–308.

Hjern, Benny, and David O. Porter. (1982). Implementation Structures: A New Unit for Administrative Analysis. *Organization Studies* 2: 211–237.

Ingram, Helen, and Dean Mann, eds. (1980). *Why Policies Succeed or Fail.* Beverly Hills, Calif.: Sage, 1980.

Kentucky Department of Environmental Protection. (1988). *Feasibility of*

Kentusky Administration of the Dredge and Fill (404) Permit Program. Frankfort: Division of Water (September).

Kirkpatirck, George C. and Hurley W. Rudd. (1991). Official correspondance to William K. Reilly, Administrator of EPA (October 8).

Lester, James P. (1994). *Environmental Politics and Policy.* Durham: Duke University Press.

Lipsky, Michael. (1971). Street–level Bureaucracy and the Analysis of Urban Reform. *Urban Affairs Quarterly* 6: 391–409.

———. (1978; 1983). *Street Level Bureaucracy.* Beverly Hills: Sage.

Lockwood, Sue. (1994). Assumption, New Jersey Style. *National Wetlands Newsletter* 16 (4): 6–7.

Lowi, Theodore J. (1972). Four Systems of Policy, Politics, and Choice. *Public Administration Review* 32: 298–310.

Luebke, Paul A. (1990). *Tarheel Politics.* Chapel Hill: University of North Carolina Press.

Manley, Robert E. 1987. Federalism and the Management of the Environment. *The Urban Lawyer* 19: 661–681.

Mazmanian, Daniel A., and Paul A. Sabatier. (1981). *Effective Policy Implementation.* Lexington: Lexington Books.

Meeks, Gordon, and L. Cheryl Runyon. (1990). *Wetlands Protection and the States.* Denver: National Conference of State Legislatures.

Michigan Department of Natural Resources. (1991). *Meeting State and National Wetlands Goals: A Wetland Conservation Strategy for Michigan.* Lansing: University Printing, Michigan State University.

Miniter, Richard. (1991). Muddy Waters: A Quagmire of Wetland Regulation. *Policy Review* 56: 70–77.

Minnesota Department of Natural Resources. (1989). *State of Minnesota Federal Section 404 Assumption Feasibility Study.* Minneapolis: Division of Waters (August 31).

Mitsch, William, and David Gosselink. (1986). *Wetlands.* New York: Van Nostrand Reinhold Company.

Mueller, Dennis. (1989). *Public Choice II.* New York: Cambridge University Press.

National Wetlands Policy Forum. (1990). *Issues in Wetlands Protection: Background Papers Prepared for the National Wetlands Policy Forum.* Washington, D.C.: The Conservation Foundation.

Nebraska Department of Environmental Control. (1982). *Report on Feasibility Study of State 404 Assumption.* Lincoln, NE: State of Nebraska.

New Jersey. (1987). *Freshwater Wetlands Protection Act of 1987.* Trenton: N.J.S.A. 13:9B-1 *et seq*, 1987.

New Jersey Administrative Code, Section 7:7A.

Nice, David C., and Patricia Frederickson. (1994). *The Politics of Intergovernmental Relations.* Chicago: Nelson-Hall.

North Carolina Department of Natural Resources and Community Development. (1986). *Report on Fesibility of State 404 Assumption.* Raleigh: Division of Planning and Assessment (March).

Oregon Division of Lands. (1988). *State Assumption of the Federal 404 Permit Process.* Salem: Oregon Division of Lands (December).

O'Toole, Laurence J. (1991). *A Feasibility Study of Management of the sections 401 and 404 Programs by the State of Alabama.* Auburn, AL: Water Resource Research Institute.

Peterson, Paul E., Barry G. Rabe, Kenneth K. Wong. (1986) *When Federalism Works.* New York: Brookings.

Pressman, Jeffrey, and Aaron Wildavsky. (1973). *Implementation.* Berkeley, Calif.: University of California Press.

Prottas, Jeffrey Manditch. (1979). *People-Processing: The Street-Level Bureaucrat in Public Service Bureaucracies.* Lexington, MA: Lexington Books.

Rabe, Barry G. (1986). *Fragmentation and Integration in State Environmental Management: Issue Report.* Washington, DC: Conservative Foundation.

Regens, James. L. (1989). Congressional Cosponsorship of Acid Rain Controls. *Social Science Quarterly* 70: 505–512.

Rhoads, Steven F. (1985). *The Economist's View of the World : Governments, Markets, and Public Policy.* New York: Cambridge University Press.

Ringquist, Evan P. (1993). *Environmental Protection at the State Level : Politics and Progress in Controlling Pollution.* New York: M. E. Sharpe.

Ripley, Randall B., and Grace P. Franklin. (1982). *Bureaucracy and Policy Implementation.* Homewood, Ill.: Dorsey Press.

Ritchie, Bruce. (1997). Florida Wetlands Program Doomed, Group Charges. *http://sunone.com* (July 9).

Rooney, The Honorable John E. (1994). Personal correspondance (May 18).

Rose, Douglas H. (1973). National and Local Forces in State Politics: The Implications of Multilevel Policy Analysis. *American Political Science Review,* 67: 1162–1173.

Rose-Ackerman, Susan. (1995). Pollution and Federalism. In *Controlling Environmental Policy: The Limits of Public Law in Germany and the United States* 37–54.

Sabatier, Paul A. (1973). State and Local Government. Policy Studies Journal 1: 217–226.

———. (1983). Policy Implementation. In Stuart Nagel (ed.,) *Encyclopedia of Policy Studies.* New York: Marcel Dekker.

Sabatier, Paul A., and David Mazmanian. (1979). The Conditions of Effective Implementation: A Guide to Accomplishing Policy Objectives. *Policy Analysis* 5: 481–504.

———. (1980). The Implementation of Public Policy: A Framework for Analysis. *Policy Studies Journal* 8: 538–560.

South Carolina Department of Health and Environmental Control. (1986). *A Feasibility Study of Assumption of the Section 404 Program by the State of South Carolina.* Columbia: Division of Water Quality and Shellfish Sanitation (December).

Swanson, Kathleen O., and James Stoutamire. (n.d.) *Permit Data Sharing Between the Florida Department of Environmental Protection and the Regional Water Management Districts.* Tallahassee: Florida Department of Environmental Protection, http:// www.dep.state.fl/eris/erpds/paper.html.

Switzer, Jacqueline Vaughn. (12993). *Environmental Politics: Domestic and Global Dimensions.* New York: St. Martin's.

Tidwell, Greer C. (1991) Official correspondance to Senator George C. Kirkpatirck and Representative Hurley W. Rudd. (December 23).

US Army Corps of Engineers. (1997). *Public Notice 97–17: Suspension of the Nationwide Permits (NWPs) in Maryland.* Baltimore: USACE Baltimore District Office.

U.S. Environmental Protection Agency. (1992). *Final Report: Study of State Assumption of the Section 404 Program.* Washington, D.C.: U.S. Environmental Protection Agency (October 23).

———. (1990). *Report of Audit: Wetlands: Region 4 Implementation of the Section 404 Wetlands Program.* Atlanta: Office of the Inspector General, Region 4 (March 23).

———. (1991). *Report of Audit: Wetlands: EPA's Implementation and Management of the Section 404 Wetlands Program.* Washington, D.C.: Office of the Inspector General, (September 30).

Van Horne, Carl, and Donald Van Meter. (1976). The Implementation of Intergovernmental Policy. In Charles O. Jones and Robert Thomas (eds.) *Public Policy Making in the Federal System.* Beverly Hills: Sage.

Van Meter, Donald, and Carl Van Horne. (1975).The Policy Implementation Process: A Conceptual Framework. *Administration and Society* 6: 445–488.

White House, Executive Office of the President. (1993). *Protecting America's Wetlands: A Fair, Flexible, and Effective Approach.* Washington, D.C.: White House Office on Environmental Resources (August).

Wisconsin Department of Natural Resources. (1991). *An Assessment of Wisconsin's Wetland Protection Programs: Should the State Assume the Federal Wetland Fill Permit Program?* Madison: Bureau of Water Regulation and Zoning.

Wise, Charles, and Rosemary O'Leary. (1997). Intergovernmental Relations and Federalism in Environmental Managements and Policy: the Role of the Courts. *Public Administration Review* 57: 150–159.

Wood, Lance D. (1989). The Forum's Resommendation to Delegate Section 404 to the States: A Bad deal for Wetlands. *National Wetlands Newsletter* 11(July–August): 2–5.

World Wildlife Fund. (1992). *Statewide Wetlands Strategies: A Guide to Protecting and Managing the Resource.* Washington, D.C.: Island Press, 1992.

Zawitoski, Gina. (1997). *Wetlands Protection in Maryland.* Baltimore: Piper and Marbury LLP, http://www.pipernar.com/article32.html.

Index